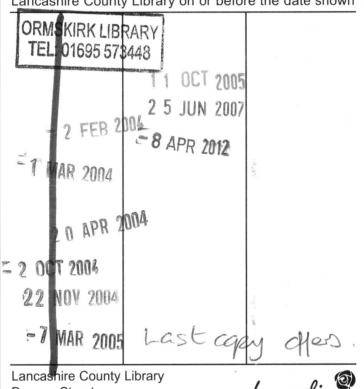

ENCYCLOPEDIA OF
MOSAIC

ENCYCLOPEDIA OF
MOSAIC

ELAINE M. GOODWIN

BT BATSFORD

0914378742

I should like to pay my personal respects to three mosaic authorities to whom I am deeply in debt and who are now no longer with us: Arthur Goodwin who initiated me into the mechanics and mysteries of the mosaic medium; Peter Fischer whose mosaic-filled friendship was both feisty and fun; and Jeanne Reynal who, above all, was a mosaicist's mosaicist – a truly modern pioneer.

First published 2003

Text © Elaine M. Goodwin 2003

The right of Elaine M. Goodwin to be identified as Author of this work has been asserted by her in accordance with the Copyright, Designs and Patents Act 1988.

ISBN 07134 8777 1

A CIP catalogue record for this book is available from the British Library.

Volume © B T Batsford

Printed and bound by Kyodo Printing (Singapore) Pte Ltd

for the publishers

B T Batsford
The Chrysalis Building
Bramley Road
London W10 6SP

www.batsford.com

A member of Chrysalis Books plc

Image on title page: *Serenissima III*, 2002 by Elaine M Goodwin, 50cm x 50cm/20in x 20in, Venetian gold, smalti, platinum, mirror, marble, ceramic (JM).

Introduction

This is a book for the mosaic enthusiast, both practitioner and appreciator. To enjoy and understand contemporary mosaic, whether as a specialist or devotee, it is enlightening to know something of its long and brilliant history, through the Classical, Byzantine, Victorian and twentieth-century eras to arrive at the present.

I have, therefore, gathered Greek, Latin, Spanish, Arabic, Italian and French terminology where relevant, as aids for research into this tradition. These terms will enable identification on archaeological sites that hold mosaics, and inform research in museums, books and galleries. They will also help in recognizing and classifying motifs for use in studio work.

Some past terms have come into general use in mosaic making, e.g., *tessera*, *andamento*, *emblema*, etc., but some words have accrued ambiguities or meanings at variance with present-day understanding or are not used in the same context as they were previously – mosaic historians have differed! I have tried to clarify terms as they are understood today by myself and leading practitioners and authorities. General art terms are explained with a particular emphasis or specific reference to mosaic.

This is very much a book for use today, illustrated with work from artists working world-wide, mostly professionals, who are acclaimed in their field. This is so that readers can become inspired as well as informed about what is happening now, in the twenty-first century, when what could have become an archaic art form is instead an invigorated and innovative medium, as profound and permanent as her sister arts of sculpture and painting.

I am aware that this is the first mosaic encyclopaedia of this century, and as such, all omissions and opinions fall to me – forgive me for any lacunae and inaccuracies. I am sure you will inform me of improvements and additions.

Acknowledgements

My thanks to my fellow artists, mosaic friends and colleagues who, although from many countries, all speak the same language; my travelling friends who have joined me on classical sites and at Byzantine edifices and on many a 'mosaic' adventure; my students who delight me with their enthusiasm and innovation, and to David Harvey, classicist and friend, for his expertise and 'read through'. Most importantly, especial thanks to my long-suffering friends Lindy Ayubi, interpreter of my unintelligible scribblings to presentable disk, and John Melville, for tireless patience and sparkling photography; also to Nick and Rosie Melville, for digital translation of my paper drawings; and to my sons Rama Mark and Darius Alexander, who keep my feet firmly on the ground.

ABACULUS (pl. **abaculi**; Gk. *abakiskos*) One of the names given to a cube of stone, glass or other material used in the making of mosaics. **See *tessellae; tessera.***

ABACUS (pl. **abaci**; Gk. *abax*) The tray used in the making of a mosaic *emblema* in Greco–Roman times. It is usually made of terracotta, marble, stone or travertine.

ABBOZZO (It.) A rough drawing or sketch; the first markings or jottings for a later work.

ABSTRACT A mosaic that has no representative (i.e. figurative) or naturalistic motifs, relying for its force on colour, form, line or movement. **See *non-representational.***

ACANTHUS A very popular plant motif used in Classical and Byzantine mosaics and architecture. Acanthus scrolls are found, depicted in mosaic with great virtuosity, in borders and friezes and as a central 'tree' motif on floors and apses. **See *arbor vitae.***

Abstract
Trittico (Silver and Violet), 1999 by Lucio Orsoni, approx. 300cm x 140cm / 118in x 55in when displayed; white gold and smalti. (Artist's collection.)

The Venetian artist (b. 1939) is a graduate of the Accademia di Belle Arti in Venice, Italy. Lucio Orsoni occupies a unique position in the mosaic world, being both a maker and international supplier of the mosaic materials of smalti and gold leaf mosaic, and also an artist *par excellence* in his materials. His works are severely abstract, relying on the innate beauty of handmade materials and purity of concept.

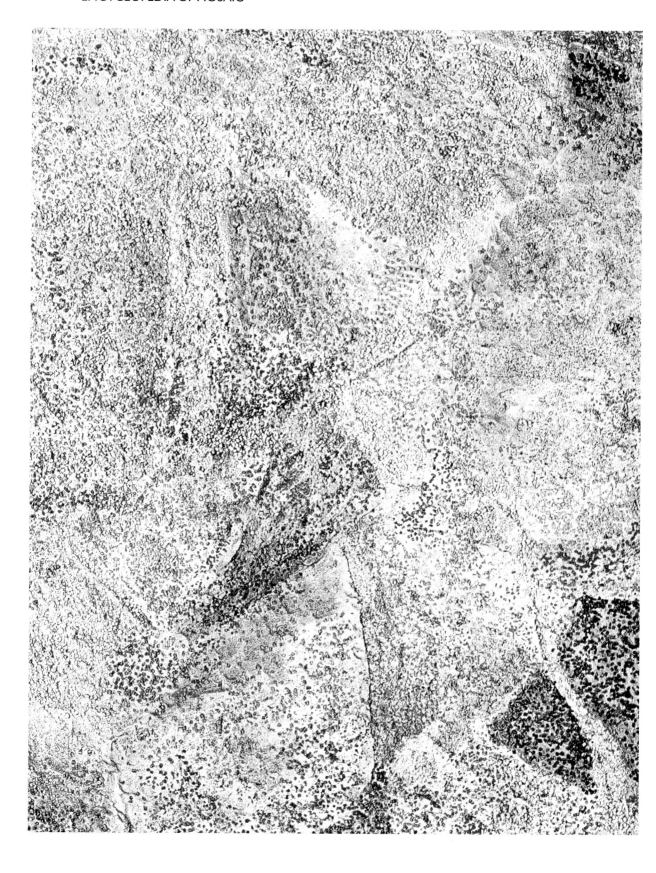

Action mosaic
Pastel Sonata, 1956–57 by Jeanne Reynal, University of Syracuse, New York, USA, 152cm x 122cm / 60in x 48in, smalti, marble on magnesite.

The New York artist (b. 1905) was a pupil of Boris Anrep in Paris, France, from 1950 to 1958. After her return to the USA, until her death, Jeanne Reynal experimented with both two-dimensional and three-dimensional mosaic work. She was a friend of many leading artists of the time, e.g. Arshile Gorky, Mark Rothko, and the de Koonings. Much travelled in Greece and Italy, she digested the fundamental elements of mosaic making for translation into modern materials. Using a variety of tools, she often drew on a coloured base of magnesite or Portland cement into which the tesserae were dribbled or dropped, and finally tapped into place to leave irregular angles. Though the technique was seemingly random, great control was achieved in the cutting and placing.

ACCENT An emphasis on one area of the mosaic. This is usually done by stressing one or more of the design elements, e.g. line, colour, etc. **See** *composition; design elements*.

ACCIDENTALS In mosaic terms these are 'enhancing tesserae' introduced into the backgrounds of mainly decorative mosaics. They can introduce colour, texture, light-reflecting materials and other accents of interest to enliven or add surprise to an otherwise uniform surface. The term can also have a more specific reference to accidental results from kiln firings, which are then used in a positive way.

ACETONE A liquid solvent used as a cleaning agent for epoxy resins. It is used to clean tools, brushes and surfaces and is followed by a thorough soap and hot water wash.

ACRYLIC GROUT ADDITIVE This is normally added to the grout for mosaics in external positions, or where more flexibility in a concrete mix is required. In a liquid form it is used instead of water; Primal AC33 is one such binder. Any colour grout is added in a powder form to the dry mortar before mixing. However, many cement adhesives in powder form have additives already incorporated in the right proportions as part of their mix. **See** *admix*.

ACTION MOSAIC A mosaic style developed at the time of action painting in the 1950s. This is where mosaic fragments of glass smalti or other materials are 'dribbled' or loosely dropped on to a prepared bed of fresh cement in a seemingly random fashion.

ADHESIVE FILM This is a transparent adhesive support material for holding tesserae in place when lifting a mosaic from a temporary base to a permanent site. It can be used in the direct method in making a mosaic on a base of sand/clay. When the mosaic is completed, apply the film using equal pressure to make sure each tessera is held in place on the sheet. Lift and carefully reposition in a freshly prepared cement base. When the cement has hardened, the film can be peeled off and the surface grouted if necessary.

ADHESIVES Adhesives used in mosaic making are many. Two big divisions are those adhesives used for a temporary bond and those used for a permanent bond. Temporary adhesives are used mostly in the indirect method of setting mosaics, and are (1) flour and water; and (2) gums or pastes. These are all water-based glues. (3) Rubber-based glues and (4) adhesive film (which is self-adhesive and colourless) can be used for indirect or direct mosaic setting, and are removed by peeling. Permanent adhesives are generally waterproof and are (1) impact or contact glues; (2) tile-setting cements; (3) epoxy resins; and (4) PVA (which can be waterproofed when mixed with cement).

ADMIX These are liquid additives supplementing a mix of sand and cement that aid malleability and lessen the drying time, reducing shrinkage and cracking. They are now generally included in the dry cement mix as part of its powder form.

ADVANCING COLOURS Hot or bright colours appear to come forward from the surface or move closer to the viewer; these are often pure red, yellow and orange.

Alabaster
Three in one, 1993 by Elaine M Goodwin, 36cm x 36cm
/ 14in x 14in, smalti, Venetian gold, alabaster chippings.
(Private collection) (JM)

One of a series of mosaics made by the author in the
early 1990s after extensive visits to Egypt. The
alabaster was from Karnak temple, Luxor, and has
associations with life/death.

Aluminium mesh
The Kennedy Memorial, 1968 by Kenneth Budd, St Chad's, Birmingham City Centre, England, 18.5m x 5m / 66ft x 16ft, smalti, glass mosaic.

The artist Kenneth Budd devised a direct setting technique which he employed on large-scale works from the 1960s until his death at the end of the 20th century. This involved covering a cartoon of the complete work, which was vertically mounted in his studio in Penge, near London, with aluminium mesh. The mosaic was then set using a flexible adhesive mortar. When complete, the work was dismounted in 1m² sections, and re-erected on site. When fully assembled, the joints between the panels were 'made good' and the work grouted. In this way large-scale works could be made in the direct method with no visible joins. This is a technique that has been slightly modified and is used by his son Oliver today.

AESTHETIC Anything pertaining to the beautiful, tasteful, artistic or refined.

AFRICANUM See *opus africanum.*

AGATE A variety of quartz, usually banded in concentric circles of colour. It can range from blue to warm orange. **See *stones (precious/semiprecious).***

'AGED' LIME Lime is used in mosaic as a binder in a mortar of sand and cement. It has three purposes: (1) to make the mix more malleable; (2) to slow the curing or hardening process of the mortar; (3) to reduce the shrinkage of the mortar as it cures.

Procedure: mix lime powder and water in a plastic container to a creamy consistency; leave. When the water rises and appears on the surface, pour it off. After a few days the mix will have a very malleable, dough-like feel. Use it in this state, or leave it to dry and crumble to a fine powder for storage and later use. The proportions required are generally 1 cement : 3/4 sand : 1 'aged' lime. **See *lime; lime putty.***

AGGREGATE This is an inert material, like gravel, rubble, crushed rock, or crushed stone. It is used bound with sand, lime, cement and water to form concrete. Aggregates range from a very fine powder form, which may include marble dust, to large lumps of stone. They are added to strengthen a mix of mortar, and also add texture and sometimes colour.

AGIA (ayia) / AGIOS (ayios) The Greek terms for the female and male saints in Byzantine and Christian churches.

ALA (pl. **alae**) 'Wing' or 'wings' of a Roman villa. These are living rooms or small waiting rooms opening on to the atrium on each side of the tablinum (dining room), and often have a mosaic floor.

ALABASTER A translucent stone of white or off-white colour, often used in a ground or crushed form in mosaic making.

ALEXANDRINUM See *opus alexandrinum*.

ALUMINIUM MESH A strong, fine and expanded metal mesh of grid formation that is used as a reinforcing material for making mosaics on a larger scale. It can also be cut to size and used in making smaller cement slabs, to give strength and rigidity. This is particularly useful in external paving features. It is also known as expanded metal mesh.

ALUMINOUS CEMENT A hydraulic cement that resists water. It is made by mixing limestone and bauxite (which contains a high proportion of alumina) and sets very quickly to a high strength. It is good for emergency works and small repairs to mosaics. Varieties include *ciment fondu* (dark grey) or Secar 71 (white).

ANDAMENTO (It. *andare*, to walk, to go) The visual movement of the tesserae on the mosaic surface, which emphasizes the flow or coursing of the tesserae e.g. around a contour, or in a background. It gives movement and rhythm, and may be circular, horizontal, sinuous etc. It can also mean the movement of the eye over a mosaic. **See *flow.***

ANDRON (pl. **andrones**) The dining room in a Greek house or Roman villa. It is square or rectangular, with room for three or more dining couches. In Greek architecture it denoted the men's quarters where the owner of the house entertained formally. They often have high quality mosaics. Superb pebble examples can be seen in Greece, at Eretria, 4th century BC.

Andamento
Exposure I, 2000 by Elaine M Goodwin, 66cm x 127cm / 26in x 50in, Venetian gold, smalti, iron pyrites. (Collection of J Balfour-Paul; JM)

The movement of the tesserae is highly controlled in this work, one of two on the same theme. The andamento emphasizes the nature of the theme in a series of 'revealing' movements.

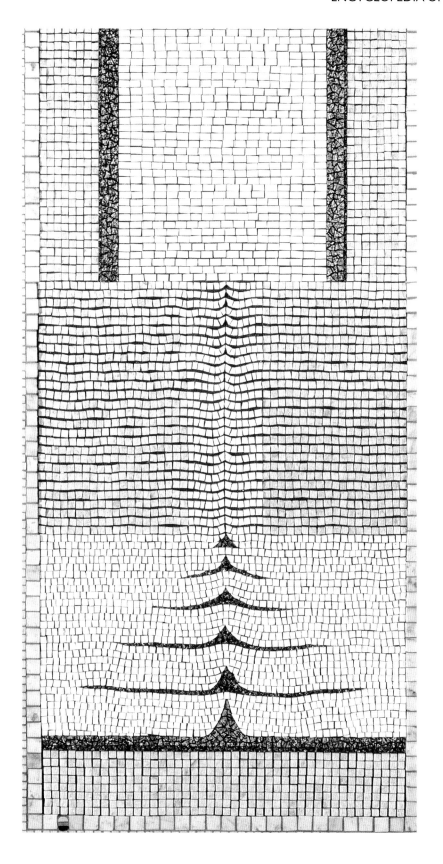

ANGLE GRINDER A tool used to cut and carve stone. A good manageable size is 10cm / 4in. It should be fitted with stone-cutting and/or grinding discs. Use a vice or pliers to hold the stone steady, and wear eye protection when in action.

ANGLE OF TESSERAE Mosaic tesserae may be set at an angle or tilted into the bedding adhesive to make optimum play of available light. The tesserae may be pressed at any angle towards or away from a light source. **See *setting tesserae.***

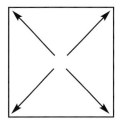

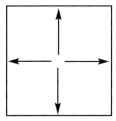

The tesserae may be pressed at any angle – towards or away from a light source.

ANIMA (L. 'air, spirit, soul'). In mosaic-glassmaking terms, this wonderful word is used for a half-worked, low-melting glass colorant and opacifier for transparent glass. Thus the 'souls' are specially prepared and added to the transparent colourless or coloured glass.

ANNEALING A controlled process of gradual cooling of the molten glass in the glass furnace – or at other stages of glass preparation – to eliminate any strain created in the making of the glass. **See *smalto/smalti.***

ANNULAR VAULT A curved walkway or processional walkway covered by an arched vault or ceiling that may be covered with mosaic. A supreme example is Santa Costanza, mid-4th century AD, Rome, Italy, built as the mausoleum of Constantine's daughter, Constantina.

APODYTERIUM The undressing room in a Roman bathhouse (*thermae*).

APPLIED DECORATION Decoration or ornament applied to a surface. Mosaic is often referred to as a medium of applied decoration, particularly when describing decorative mosaics and those made for garden and interior settings.

APSE A semicircular space at the end of a hall or basilica. There are innumerable wonderful examples of churches decorated with mosaics in this space, e.g. S Apollinare (6th century AD) in Classe, Ravenna, Italy, and Hosios David (late 5th century AD), Thessaloniki, Greece.

ARABESQUES Decorative forms composed of flowing lines, depicting plant tendrils or vegetal forms, often as part of an interlaced design. This form of organic, often linear, design is used a lot in decorative mosaics. **See *decorative mosaic; ornamental composition.***

ARBOR VITAE Tree of Life; a popular motif for mosaics from early Byzantine times. When a symbol of the cross is included in the design this becomes a Cross-Arbor Vitae; a fine example is the apse mosaic of San Clemente, 12th century AD, Rome, Italy. In this case the 'tree' is a spiralling acanthus plant. **See *Tree of Life*.**

ARCHITECTURAL FAIENCE (glazed terracotta) During the 19th century, this consisted of moulded or cast slabs of fired or glazed clay, which were used as a decorative form of cladding.

ARMATURE A framework or support for a structure. To create a three-dimensional or freestanding mosaic sculpture it may be necessary to buy or make an armature. Bought armatures may have sliding parts, with adjustable arms to support and underpin the mosaic, and may also incorporate screw-holes for fixing the work to a base. These are excellent for 3D work when modelling in cement. They may also be constructed of wood or metal to the basic shape needed. Chicken wire or aluminium wire can then be utilized to build up a required simple form. This is then covered with scrim or fine gauze, impregnated with a cement slurry. When set, this is further 'gloved', worked on with a trowel or by hand to a smooth finished surface ready to take a mosaic. The final slurry coat can be brushed on to create a smoother continuous surface. **See *glass fibre mesh.***

Arabesques
Awakened Night, 2001 by Elaine M Goodwin, 105cm x 92cm / 41in x 36in, ceramic, silver leaf mosaic, platinum-glazed ceramic, vitreous glass. (Artist's collection; JM)

A decorative panel using a restrained palette of black, white, silver and colourless glass to throw into relief the arabesque nature of a highly ornamental design. By introducing a central motif, the organic forms can entwine and encircle about a static centrepiece for even greater decorative effect.

ARMATURE WIRE / ALUMINIUM WIRE A flexible wire used to build a 3D structure on the armature. It can be of varying strength and malleability, and used for interior and exterior work. The thickness can be varied according to the dexterity required in creating the form and the strength of the structure needed. The wire is also popularly used to hang mosaics from walls, secured between two screw eyes, staples or nails in the back of the work.

ARTISTS' PIGMENTS There are some lime-proof pigments that retain their colour when mixed with cement or lime. They are particularly good for adding colour to grout. These include Cadmium red, Vermilion and Brown, Cobalt violet, blue and turquoise, Cerulean blue, Chromium oxide, Caput mortuum, Red ochre, Indian red, Mars red, yellow and violet, Venetian red, Green earth light, Burnt green earth, Terre verte, Golden ochre and Yellow ochre, and Raw umber. They are all permanent. Other artists' pigments, including pearl lustres, which are made from mica flakes, can also be used for tile grouts – experiment! They are also light-fast and impervious to acids and alkalis. They can add sparkling brilliance to a grout or setting bed.

ASAROTON Literally 'unswept'. A term used for a mosaic floor showing a *trompe l'oeil* design of an assemblage of scattered objects or debris, often from a dining table. The best-known examples are copies from the master mosaicist Sosus of Pergamum, who lived in the 2nd century BC in North West Asia Minor. Thus *asarotos oikos* – 'unswept house' (Greek).

ATRIUM The central hall or court of a Roman villa, in part generally open to the sky and containing an impluvium (rain catcher/water basin), and sometimes a fountain.

AVENTURINE (It. *avventura*, an adventure!) A form of glass paste with particles of copper or chromic oxide added to the vitreous glass mosaic base to give a wonderful sparkling metallic effect. **See *vitreous glass.***

AZULEJOS Spanish tiles, developed during the 12th century and still used today. Originally they were small and set into wall surfaces. **See *cuenca; cuerda seca.***

Aventurine brooch (Early 20th century)
The brooch is Italian, around 4cm / 1 1/2in diameter.
A mosaic of miniature geometric tesserae of smalti,
with sparkling gold-coloured particles added for
textural effect. The whole is polished smooth and
set in silver. A very collectable piece. (JM)

BAND SAW A useful adjunct to the studio is a table top saw with a diamond-plated banded steel blade that can be adjusted for cutting glass up to 12mm / ¹/₂ in. Some models can also cut wood and non-ferrous metals.

BAR The term for a single piece of composite glass formed by fusing together canes or rods. This is then cut into slices to form glass inlays.

BASE Backing material for a mosaic. Choosing this depends on its siting and permanence. Common bases include reinforced concrete, cement rendering, plywood, hardboard and MDF (though I personally dislike this material). Other bases or backing surfaces include those made of polyester resins, metal, steel, styrofoam, terracotta, clay and marble. Remember, a mosaic is only as durable as its base. See *supports*.

BATCH In glassmaking, this refers to the mix of raw materials, e.g. soda, lime, silica, that are heated together to make glass.

BEVEL Some materials used in mosaic making have edges cut to an oblique angle or slant. These bevelled materials can therefore be used with flexibility in three-dimensional works or when corners or angled edges are required. Most machine-made commercial vitreous tesserae, which are manufactured in uniform trays, have their four edges pre-bevelled. A bevelling machine can be used to create bevels on glass and ceramic tesserae. It sometimes comes as an attachment to a grinding machine, and will include an adjustable bevel wheel adapter, with a diamond cutting wheel. It is interesting to note that the earliest-known tesserae had bevelled or cone-shaped sides (**see Uruk**), and occasional Greek and Roman mosaic tesserae have

bevelled edges, which aided ease of placing in a setting bed. **See *glass bevels*.**

BIANCO-SOPRA-BIANCO (It. 'white over white') Developed in Bristol, England during the 18th century, this is a technique in tile making allowing details painted in pure white to show to great subtle effect on the bluish-white ground of the tile's surface.

BINDERS These are substances that help join other substances together either through a chemical reaction or by absorbing moisture. Binders most commonly used in mosaic work are cements, lime, plasticizers and resins. **See *lime plaster; lime putty*.**

BISCUIT TILE A once-fired tile of a fixed shape and size, that is undecorated and unglazed.

BITUMINOUS GLUE An organic adhesive or binder, made from petroleum deposits. It was used by the Sumerians in the fourth and third millennia BC as an adhesive for mosaics on a wood base. A fine example is the so-called Standard of Ur in the British Museum, England, 3rd millennium BC.

BLOWING A glass-making technique, created by inflating a gathering or 'gob' of molten glass on the end of a hollow iron tube or blowpipe.

BONE PINS Kiln furniture such as these are sometimes used in stone mosaics.

BOW FILE A tool for cutting or incising hard materials. The handle of the bow is made from steel or wood with an attached iron wire rubbed with emery that is used wetted with water. The emery, which is an abrasive of corundum plus ferric oxide, cuts into the hard surface.

Bevel
Obelisk (detail), part of a triptych Liquid Gold, 2001 by Elaine M Goodwin, The Eden Project, St Austell, Cornwall, England. (JM)

The materials for the base of the sculpture and the shaft were ceramic tiles and Venetian gold-leaf tesserae respectively. To enable a 'good edge' on all four sides of the free-standing work, the materials had to be bevelled at a 45° angle to give a good fit at the joins. A diamond band saw was used for the bevel and each cut surface was hand-rubbed smooth, using a diamond abrasive pad.

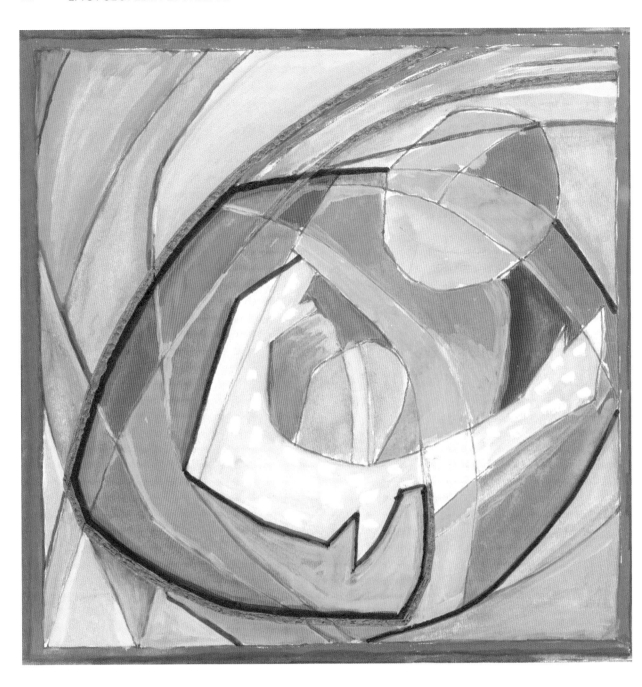

Bozzetto
The Prodigal Son, 1990–91 by Hildegart Nicholas, Chapel of
Bournemouth General Hospital, England. (JM)

The German artist Hildegart Nicholas (1913–95) was born in Bonn
and studied interior architecture at the School of Pure and Applied
Art in Munich, Germany. In the late 1960s she became a pupil of
Hans Unger in London. Her work relied on a symbiosis of colour,
luminosity and dynamic strength. All her work was deeply spiritually
motivated. For this commission she worked on approximately 30
sketches in pencil, pen and ink, and colour washes, each sketch
evolving the given theme. The colour *bozzetto* or 'mock-up' allowed
the artist to gain an idea of colour relationships, building up colour
against colour like a musical chord. The finished mosaic was made
on a marine plywood base in four panels, fortified with battens at
the back.

BOZZETTO A small sketch, painting or model used as a guide to creating a finished piece, or to show to a prospective client. It is usually made on a reduced scale and often in complete detail and colour. **See** *abbozzo; maquette.*

BREEZE BLOCKS Lighter weight building blocks that can be used as an armature and then cemented over for mosaic. They are especially good for large-scale seating, playground designing etc., when large areas need to be designed cheaply and quickly. They are also known as cinderblocks.

BRONZE The metal produced from the mixing of copper and tin.

BRUSHES There is a variety, for a variety of uses. Paint brushes or artists' brushes are used for designing and colour-washing the cartoon. Tracing brushes called 'riggers' are used for transposing drawings and drawing lines. Scrub brushes are used for removing particles from the mosaic surface, and a polishing brush is used for cleaning. Always keep at hand a dustpan and brush, bench brush or fitches for cleaning up the work top, and keep a few mop brushes for cleaning around. Floor brushes are crucial for maintaining a clear floor. Use a wire brush for cleaning off any oxidation appearing on metal, etc.; masonry brushes are invaluable for cleaning away excess cement from larger or external mosaics and great for buffing up completed large-scale mosaics.

BUBBLES Pockets of gas trapped in the glass during its making.

BUILDER'S SPONGE (tiler's sponge; grout sponge) A manufactured sponge of dense material that is very absorbent. When wetted and squeezed, it is ideal for soaking the back of papered mosaics when using the reverse or indirect method of mosaic making.

BURLAP See *gauze fabric; hessian.*

BUTTERING The application of adhesive to the back or setting side of individual tesserae.

BYZANTINE (adj., from Byzantium) The name given to the period known as the **Byzantine Empire**, which lasted from the inauguration of the capital Constantinople (Byzantium) on 11 May 330 until the capture of the city by the Ottomans on 29 May 1453, and to the style of its art. During the 4th century AD, Constantinople replaced Rome as the administrative centre of the Roman Empire (AD 476 fall of Rome).

BYZANTINE MOSAIC An art form created over a millennium, from AD 330 to the 15th century, of a primarily religious nature and found in Europe, Western Asia and North Africa. Byzantine mosaic art is often defined by its dynasties, e.g. Justinianic, Macedonian, Comnenian and Paleologian. The artists understood many of the 'modern' aspects of art, e.g. colour, colour saturation, and broken colour and eye mixing, i.e. the placing of two or more colours to produce the optical effect of a third. Great monuments to visit to see Byzantine mosaic in all its early splendour (5th–7th century) are found in the city of Ravenna in north-east Italy, and in Rome. For later wonders visit the 12th-century church mosaics of Sicily in the cities of Palermo, Cefalù and Monreale; and Greece for the 11th-century monasteries of Hosios Loukas in Phocis and Daphni, west of Athens. These are but a few of the superb examples remaining depicting the beauty and power of the art of Byzantine mosaic.

Byzantine Mosaic
'Theodora' panel (detail), San Vitale, Ravenna, Italy, mid-6th century AD. (EMG)

This detail from one of the two mosaic panels representing the Emperor Justinian and his consort, the Empress Theodora, is from the latter's entourage. The emergence of a Byzantine style is in part characterized by a sumptuous delight in texture and rich coloration, which is enhanced by the play of light on the irregular hand-cut glass material called smalti, which dematerialized the architectural walls to give heightened wonder. The colour palette is small; reds, golds, greens and whites. The complementaries of red and green are enhanced by close proximity and superb compositional control, e.g. the draperies and the female heads.

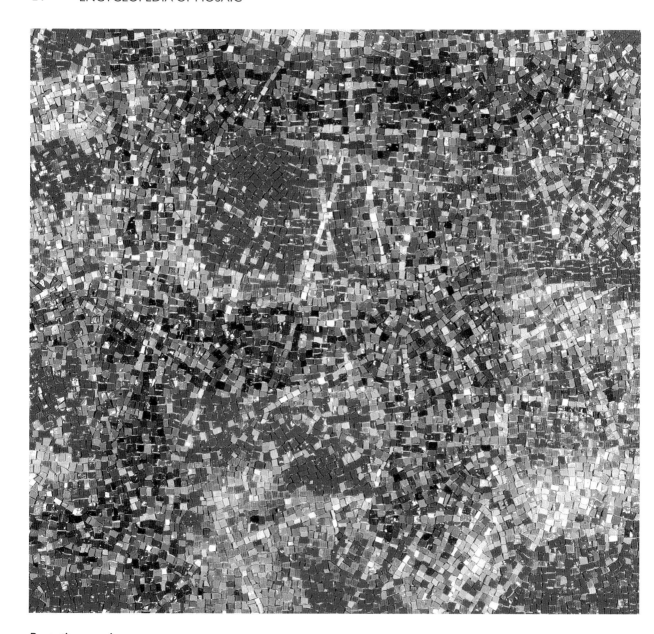

Byzantine mosaic
Cielo, 2001 by Lino Linossi, 95cm x 100cm / 37in x 39in, smalti.

An Italian artist (b. 1957) who has lived and worked in Germany since 1975, Linossi demonstrates a controlled understanding of the relationship between colour and light in the mosaic medium. He exploits in works of both a 2D and 3D nature the luminosity achievable by resonating one tessera with another, as did the mosaic masters of early Byzantium.

CAEMENTICUM See *opus caementicum.*

CABLE PATTERN A simple pattern with a twisted cord or rope-like effect, used frequently in ancient Greek and Roman mosaics. **See *guilloche.***

CALIDARIUM In a Roman bath house, this is a room in the thermae with hot pools.

CALM (L. *calamus*, reed) A grooved strip of lead that is used to join together different sections in stained glass. Also known as 'came', 'cane'. **See *lead strips.***

CANE A slender rod or bar of glass that, when cut into sections, is used in miniature mosaics. **See *filato/filati.***

CANE MOSAIC A mould or matrix made of canes of opaque glass, which are often ground and polished. It was a popular material in the 1st century AD. Canes can be shaped (e.g. square, star pattern, diamond, spiral), or pre-formed and fused in a mould. Some examples can be seen in the Victoria and Albert Museum, London, England.

Cable pattern
Cable pattern (detail), Ancient Dion, Greece 2nd/3rd century AD. (EMG)

A pavement showing in the centre a fine example of a simple black and white cable pattern; a meander to the left and a design made up of peltae to the right. The damaged floor shows clearly in the foreground the individual cubes or tesserae and to the far left, larger irregular stone border tessellation.

Cartellina
A collection of 8cm / 3in slabs of Venetian gold metallic leaf. In each case the cartellina or thin covering glass has been coloured, before the application of the 24 carat gold leaf or white gold/silver leaf. Notice that in some cases the surface is not plain or smooth but granulated.
(JM)

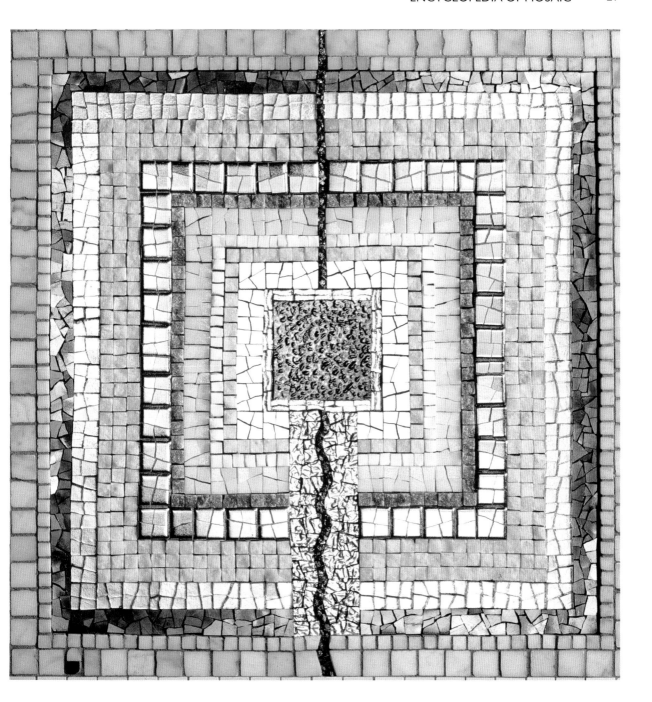

Cartellina
Summum Bonum, 2001 by Elaine M Goodwin, 50cm x 50cm / 20in x 20in, Venetian gold, smalti, Venetian reverse gold, ceramic, glazed ceramic.
(Collection of P Blundell-Jones.) (JM)

The resonant colour in this work by the author is a green metallic gold, the result of a coloured cartellina. The colour gives reference to the paradisial nature of the work. Each surface, whether matt, metallic, glazed or reflective, is played to maximum effect, as each element of the work has equal importance.

CARBON STEEL HAND TOOLS These are used for breaking down large rocks or stones. Examples are stone chisels of both heavy and light duty that are very good for breaking through slate and schist and stone. Tungsten-tipped chisels are used for limestone and granite – after which the hammer and hardie can be employed to cut the material into tesserae. **See** *hardie.*

CARBORUNDUM A crystalline compound of carbon and silicone used for smoothing, grinding, sharpening, and polishing stones and pebbles; or for sharpening tools. It is found in stone or powder form; emery is a type of carborundum. **See** *finish; grinding wheel.*

CARDO MAXIMUS This is the main street crosswise of a Roman city. **See also** *decumanus maximus*

CARPET PATTERN An all-over design (often repetitive) of freely distributed forms. Wonderful examples are found in Madaba and Mount Nebo in Jordan (7th, 8th century). **See** *opus musivum.*

CARTELLINA This term, sometimes also called 'vetrino', refers to the covering glass on gold and silver metallic tesserae. It is usually 0.2–1mm / $^1/_{20}$in thick, except for floor gold glass, which can be up to 10mm / $^3/_8$in thick. The glass is there to protect the metal leaf from oxidation, and it can be coloured to give 'coloured' golds. The metal is applied to the glass and is then fired in a kiln (very secret!), resulting in a secure attachment. The top glass rarely comes loose – as did tend to happen in earlier days.

CARTOON Usually a full-sized drawing for a mosaic, not a work of art in itself, but a scheme or a concept drawing to be interpreted in the carrying out of the mosaic. It is not a slavishly restrictive drawing, which would result in dull, predictable 'mosaic by numbers'.

CASTRUM A fortified citadel, seen as a motif in Classical Roman mosaics, e.g. Fishbourne, England, 1st–2nd century.

CEMENT A fundamental ingredient in mosaic making – easily available, malleable, a great adhesive, able to be coloured and cheap. It is a powder made by roasting and grinding a mixture of crushed chalk, clay or limestone. It is generally grey in colour or white. Cement is rarely used alone, its strength and adhesive properties becoming apparent when mixed with other materials. It is generally mixed with sand of varying degrees of fineness. Additives or plasticizers can be added for more malleability and longer time usage. The word 'cement' is often used to mean 'mortar', which is really a mix made up of cement, sand, water and/or lime or plasticizers. The Italian term for cement mortar is 'stucco'; it consists of 1 part brick dust, 1 part marble dust, 1 part aged lime putty and 3 parts boiled linseed oil. This is mixed and rolled out on a slab, cut into squares approx. 10cm x 10cm / 4in x 4in, and left to dry. When hard it is crushed to a powder. When ready for use, more linseed oil (1 part raw, 3 parts boiled) is carefully added to make it become like cream cheese in consistency. In use it is very malleable. Store cement in dry conditions. Should any damp get into a bag of cement and cause

Cement

Crater no. 3, 2002 by Pascale Beauchamps, 90cm x 90cm / 35in x 35in, cement, pebbles, smalti and Venetian gold leaf, vitreous glass.

A French artist, born in Paris (1952), who lives and works in Brittany. Her work frequently opens up a dialogue both between the tesserae used – found pebble and refined gold – and the ground or setting bed, which is often a large area of natural, textured or coloured cement.

Chimera

Mythological Creatures (detail of a unicorn and a chimera), 1996–97 by Elaine M
Goodwin and Group 5, St Thomas First School, Exeter, England, approx. 6m x 9m /
20ft x 30ft. (JM)

During the years 1985 to 1997 the author and her Group 5 worked on 14 mosaic
murals in the city of Exeter, England. The murals ranged from approximately 5m² to
60m² / 16sq.ft to 200sq.ft, and were mainly composed of recycled materials
donated by the citizens of Exeter, e.g. china, tiles and ceramic-ware. The theme for
each mural was specific to the site, whether school, community centre, city arcade
or multistorey car park. This mural, in an otherwise featureless area of the city, was
to add fantasy and encourage enquiry (well, it is a school!) into the legends
surrounding mythical beasts.

lumps to occur, disregard the bag (it is hygroscopic, which means it attracts water – a property to be taken account of in use, too). Cement should always feel fine and silky to the touch.

CEMENT-BASED ADHESIVE This can be either grey or white. It is a frost-proof powder developed to provide excellent adhesion in dry and wet settings. A variety of products with differing qualities are now available, which include rapid-set, exterior, and flexible (with a latex additive) adhesives; check that these have Portland cement or an equivalent as the base cement. They are generally mixed with water and trowelled on to dry surfaces for bonding. Again, read the instructions on proprietary brands and if necessary or in doubt, ring the customer advice or information line. Many established firms have experts in mosaic fixing and are pleased to divulge their knowledge. **See *flexible bonding.***

CEMENT MORTAR This was originally understood as a mortar consisting of sand, 'aged' lime and water, and is still used in mosaic work today. A tried and tested mortar uses 4 parts dry cement, 3 parts dry sand, one part aged lime (+ cement colouring). It must be mixed well together in a dry state before the water is added. There are today many dry ready-mixed cements and cement adhesives in powder form on the market, with fine/coarse sand added. Read the instructions on the bags for curing/drying/hardening times. Most are suitable for interior and exterior positions. **See *lime plaster; curing; concrete.***

CEMENT PIGMENT Special earth colours can be added to cement for coloration; they are very concentrated. They are bought under various branded names, such as Cementone, Febtone. Colours include red, green, brown, charcoal and blue. **See *pigments.***

CEMENT RECIPES Individual artists experiment with recipes, varying their ratios of sand to cement and also exploring a variety of binders. I once used sherry at Christmas when too lazy (intoxicated) to get water from the studio, and formed a very malleable, delicious-smelling mix. In St Paul's Cathedral (London, England) Sir W B Richmond used a cement recipe found in a 15th-century manuscript in Bologna, incorporating wax, lime and resin. He is known to have said it kept moist between 5–8 hours, could be worked as if it was wax, and when hard would not shrink. A cement recipe used in restoration work, as in Daphni, near Athens, Greece, was given to me recently by Demetrios Chrysopoulos: 2 parts lime, 1 part brick dust, 1 part pozzolana (volcanic ash from Santorini), 1 part sand (from the mountains), and only $1/3$ part of white Portland cement.

CERAMIC This is a material made from fired clay; *porous* examples include terracotta and bricks: *non-porous* examples include porcelain and stoneware.

CERAMIC MOSAICS These are commercially made clay tesserae of ceramic or porcelain. The colours are more muted than those of coloured glass, being natural and earth colours. They are generally cheap and easy to cut. Sizes are usually from 20mm x 20mm / $3/4$in x $3/4$in.

CERAMIC TILES These can be of any size, and have either a matt or glossy surface. Unglazed tiles are coloured evenly throughout. Glazed tiles are generally of brighter surface coloration. Soak the tiles in water before setting into cement if a better adhesion is needed, as they can be very porous and soak up any moisture from the mortar, creating a weaker bond. The tiles are generally bought as papered sheets, or increasingly on mesh, and are easily soaked off their backing with cold or hot water – not so easy are those that come with silicon-bonded joints, specially spaced for use by tile layers but difficult to remove by mosaicists for individual use; try scissors and brute force!

CHAMPLEVÉ This refers to a technique using a resin-based mastic to fill in the channels or indentations carved to form a design on a stone tile.

CHIAROSCURO 'Light-dark': i.e. an extreme tonal contrast and therefore one having a high tonal 'key'. It is often used to imply a strong source of light, or emphasis. In mosaic terms, this is when a work makes pronounced use of light and dark areas.

CHIMERA (Gk. *chimaira*; L. *chimaera*) A mythical beast, fire-breathing, with a lion's head, a head of a goat on its back and a head of a serpent at the tip of its tail. Many Greek and Roman mosaics depict the animal. There is a fine pebble example at Olynthos in northern Greece of Bellerophon mounted on Pegasus fighting the chimera (5th century BC).

CHIP MOSAIC An ancient term for a mosaic made of irregular often white chippings.

CHIP PAVEMENT A paving of unshaped pieces of marble or limestone set in mortar. **See *crusta.***

CHI-RHO (or labarum) The first two letters *chi* (X) and *rho* (P) of the Greek 'Christos' (*XPICTOC* – Christ). They are often joined in a monogram and used as an abbreviation of the name. It is also called a 'christogram', and is found on wall and sarcophagus mosaics. One unique pavement example is the Hinton St Mary mosaic, 4th century AD, now in the British Museum, which has a portrait of Christ superimposed against a christogram.

CHISEL A cutting tool of steel, often with tungsten tips with a quadrangular edge, fitted into a handle – extremely useful for cutting and also levering out errant mosaic tesserae!

CIMENT FONDU This is an aluminous cement that is quick setting (24 hours) and can be used on its own or combined with other cements. It is dark grey, although there is a white cement of similar properties called Secar 71. Colour may be added to both. When mixing up a mortar, usually in the proportion of 6 sand, 2 cement, 1 water, take care not to use too much water, which would result in the mix becoming too porous and therefore weaker. Take the usual precautions over drying, i.e. slowly and leaving well covered by plastic or soaked rags to prevent over-quick drying. Once set it hardens very rapidly and is very strong. It is ideal to use for 3D mosaic making, because the base form can be made with relative speed. **See *aluminous cement; glass fibre.***

CIPOLLINO A green and white striped marble veined like an onion (It. *cipolla*), especially that from Carystos (Euboea).

CLASSICAL MOSAIC Mosaic was a popular secular and religious form of decoration used throughout the Greek and Roman world from the 5th century BC until around AD 500 in Europe, Western Asia and North Africa. Examples include the mosaics from Pompeii and Herculaneum in Italy, before AD 79; a superb late example is the Great Palace Pavement in Istanbul, Turkey, c. 4th century AD. Mosaic was utilized for home (*domus*) villa, baths (*thermae*), and fountains (*nymphaea*). The medium was, in the main, used for floors, but also for walls, vaults, columns and niches. The designs were resplendent with gods and goddesses, sports, still-lifes, hunting and agriculture. Many artists working today have been or are greatly inspired by the imagery, technical skill and sheer virtuosity of Classical mosaics.

CLAY There are various oil-based sculpting clays available, which are non-drying and good for modelling 3D forms because their adhesive properties are excellent. Epoxy modelling clay can be carved and screwed and drilled when it has set hard, and provides a versatile base for mosaics. Polymer clay remains workable until cured/hardened in a domestic oven – after which it can be sanded and used as a base for mosaic.

CLEAVE When referring to pebbles or stones, this term implies a natural breaking.

CLOISONNÉ A technique whereby a work is partitioned or divided by metal strips set on edge (cloisons) holding an inlay or enamel.

CLOISONS (of mortar; lit. partitions) A term for the risen areas of mortar between tesserae. If these are allowed to set hard they can interfere with the smooth surface or the design. It is easy to forget to clean these away when rushing away at the end of a day's work.

COCCIO A crock, potsherd or piece of terracotta.

COCCIOPESTO (lit. pounded terracotta) Broken or crushed terracotta mixed with lime to a pinkish-red colour; used in pavements with tesserae of marble added for a design element.

COLLAGE/'MOSAIC' COLLAGE/ASSEMBLAGE A style of mosaic making that involves the assembling and adhering of materials of various properties, e.g. tiles, crockery, mosaic glass, *objets*

Cocciopesto

Cocciopesto pavement (detail), Ampurias (Empúries), North-eastern Spain, 1st century AD. (EMG)

Superb examples of this technique are found in this early Greek and Roman settlement where pavements and room foundations employed this simple but effective flooring, sometimes adding an inscription. The tesserae forming geometric designs are pressed into the broken and pounded terracotta, which was mixed with lime to form a warm red-coloured watertight flooring.

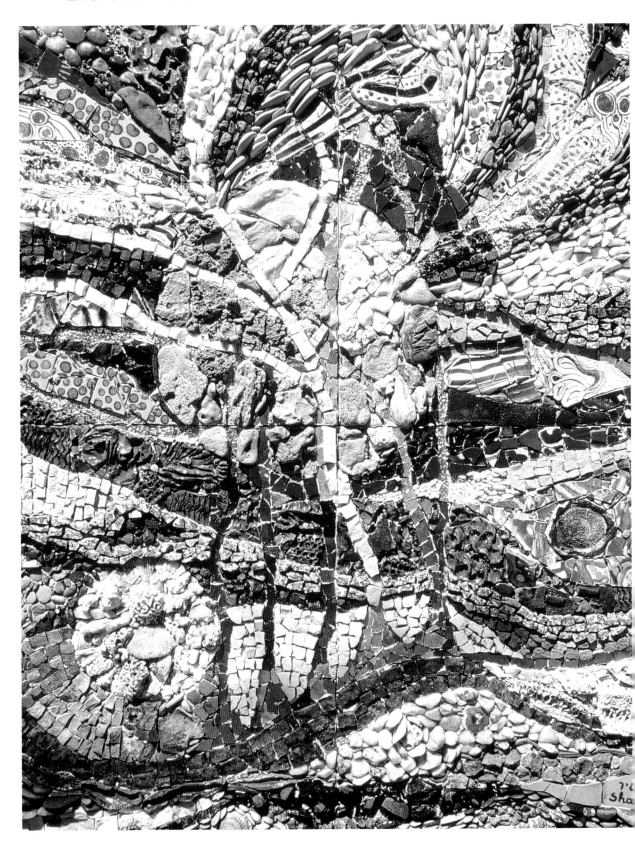

trouvés, and/or with paper, fabric etc., in creating one work – abstract or representational. Collage is usually 2D, assemblage 3D; thus a combination or mixture of a variety of materials and objects are made to form a whole.

COLOUR Hue; 'tone'. Colours can be warm, when red, yellow and orange generally predominate, or cool/cold, when blue, green and violet generally predominate. Value is the relationship of a colour to lightness or darkness; intensity is the degree of brilliance. **See *hue*.**

COLOUR GROUPING Ways of grouping colours, particularly glass and smalti, include Imperial – reds, oranges, yellow (which tend to be the most expensive); Flesh – from very light to very dark; Ordinary – greens, black, greys, browns, off white, some blues and greens and ochres; Fine – with a brilliance; pure white, blues, greens.

COLOUR HARMONY A combination of colours that 'go together'; these are often colours from the same section of the colour wheel which have a (primary) colour in common.

COLOUR SYMBOLISM The use of colour to express an emotion, religious meaning, or other symbolic interpretation.

COLOUR WHEEL A device created in 1776 by Moses Harris in England and developed in the 19th century by Michel Chevreul in France. It is a visual aid for demonstrating how pure saturated colour creates relationships between primary, secondary and tertiary colours. It is often presented as a diagram or in a circular wheel form to demonstrate colour relationships and properties.

COLOURING AGENTS Mineral oxides are common colouring agents for glass, and are light-resistant. Typical formulae include: red: gold chloride, selenium dioxide, cadmium sulphide; blue: copper oxide, cobalt oxide; yellow: iron oxide, cadmium oxide, uranium oxide; green: copper oxide, chromium oxide; black: uranium salt; white: calcium carbonate, titanic oxide. **See *smalto*.**

COMBED MORTAR BED A setting bed prepared to take a mosaic created using the indirect method. A 'toothed' scraper is used to 'take up' the unevenness. This is usually done with a 3mm / ^{1}/sin notched trowel.

COMMESSO WORK (Lat. *commissus*, sing. – put together; It. *commessi* pl. – joined together/ combined) A type of mosaic work where individually shaped pieces of marble or stone are joined together so that the joins or seams do *not*

Collage
Cosmic Streams, 2001 by Ilana Shafir, 100cm x 120cm / 39in x 47in, natural and cut stones, handmade ceramic features and tiles, Venetian gold leaf, shells and corals.

Born in Sarajevo, formerly Yugoslavia, now Bosnia, in 1924 and a student of architecture, Ilana Shafir settled in the 1950s in Ashkelon, Israel, where she continued to paint and later make mosaics. A versatile artist whose technique reflects her concepts, a slowly evolving, accumulating and combining vision paralleling her building up of materials, which may include 'accidentals' and 'imperfections' from her oven kilns alongside naturally found objects and manufactured glass and gold.

show. It is also called 'Florentine mosaic', its roots stemming from *opus sectile*. It was very popular in Florence in the time of the Medicis, although the term was not coined until later in the 16th century. **See intarsia.**

COMPLEMENTARY COLOURS Colours that are found directly opposite each other on the colour wheel, e.g. blue/orange, yellow/violet or purple, red/green. Placed next to each other they are mutually enhancing.

COMPOSITION A design; the arrangement of forms, values, lines or other elements making up the design – e.g. shape, tone, texture, colour, etc. **See accent; design.**

COMPOSITIONAL SCHEMA The underlying geometric structure of a pattern or design in any art work or medium.

COMPUTERIZED DESIGN A drawing or design that is scanned and processed by the computer. Each part is transferred into a small square that corresponds to a single tessera. Details can be enlarged or reduced. This technique can be used to help artists to examine their work before proceeding. It also helps in collating information on quantities of colours or types of tesserae, and in pricing, showing and aiding designs for commission. In total it can be of help in ordering specific materials, and when gauging size, shape and layout.

CONCH A semicircular niche topped or crowned by a quarter dome.

CONCRETE A mix of cement, sand, shingle or aggregate and water, used for external work and pools. Concrete is therefore a cement binder or hydraulic binder. The aggregate used may be sand or coarse gravel. Concrete can be coloured to look like bronze by painting it with polyester resin and bronze powder.

CONTOUR The outer edge of a motif, object, figure or form; an outline.

COPPER BANDS Strips of metal used in mosaic conservation between subdivisions of large-scale floors that have previously been cut into sections for repositioning. They are very narrow and hold both sections in place as each section is repositioned in fresh mortar. The copper is then removed and the whole grouted, with no indication of a cut fissure. This procedure can also be used for modern mosaic pavements and flooring; no release agent is needed for the copper as it does not adhere to lime mortars or cement.

COPY BOOKS Books featuring a selection of designs are known to have been widely distributed in all Roman-occupied regions from Hellenic/Classical times onwards, even though none have survived to this day. They were probably made of perishable materials like papyrus, linen, thin wooden board, or parchment, and contained a wealth of motifs and geometric designs. Prevailing similarities of design are seen, for example, in the Cirencester and Woodchester floors in England, probably stemming from the same copy book. Many mosaicists today have collected images for use from the many books available on ornamental design and

Colour harmony
Autumn Wind, 2002 by Ketty Abdel-Malek, 100cm x 90cm / 39in x 35in, Venetian gold leaf, smalti, marble, alabaster.

The Egyptian artist Ketty Abdel-Malek was born in Alexandria and trained at the Arts Academy and later in the mid-1990s at Ravenna in Italy. She has worked in many media including sculpture, woodcut and painting, and in particular mosaic. This work creates harmonies of colour of varying intensity and strikes different chords of colour that surprise and play on the eye and in the mind.

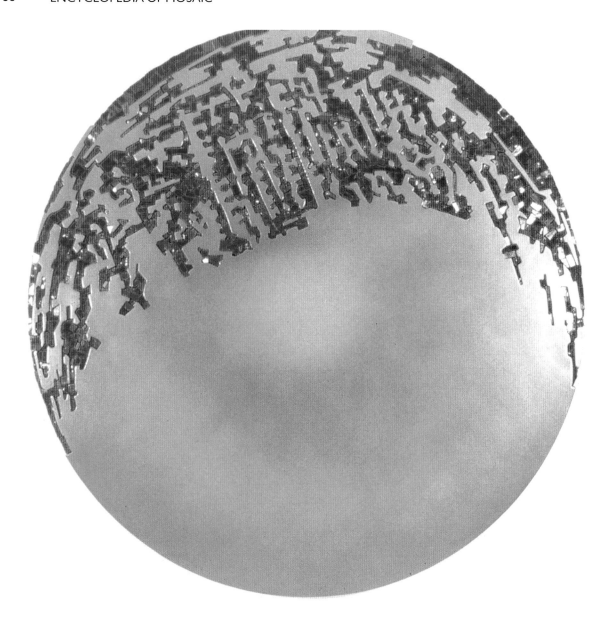

Computerized design
Red Life Disc, 1986 by Jerry W Carter, 100cm diameter x 3cm width / 39in diameter x
1in width on a cast synthetic stone.

The American artist Jerry W Carter (b. 1941) was born in Kansas and lives and works in
Silver Spring, Maryland USA. He studied mosaic at the Accademia di Ravenna in Italy and
in the 1980s was one of the international artists who participated in a grand artistic
project of urban renewal in Ravenna – the Parco della Pace, or Park of Peace – where
he created a seminal work, *La Secunda Genesi*, an external free-standing mural on the
eternal themes of life and death. In his work of the 1980s and into the early 1990s the
artist used the computer to design many of his mosaic works. The mosaic illustrated
was drawn on a digital board using a digital stylus. The glaze uses a combination of
enamels after the painting style of the early Venetian painters.

non-copyright design imagery made available for art work. **See *pattern books; repertory.***

COSMATESQUE or **COSMATINE MOSAIC** A form of mosaic, probably inspired by Arab work seen in Sicily, that is made up of highly coloured geometric designs for partial decoration on door posts, porches, architraves, pulpits, candelabra, columns and pavements, etc. The multicoloured mosaics are flat and make much use of gold leaf for brilliant reflection, and also marble, often red porphyry, green serpentine and white marble. Shapes included triangular, circular, trapezoidal, lozenge and square tesserae of marble, cut and joined into myriad repeated patterns, e.g. star shapes. The work was produced by Roman artists from the period of Pope Gregory VII (1073–85) until Pope Honorius III (1216–27), but interest was reawakened in the 19th and early 20th centuries. It is also called flat polychrome geometric mosaic, Byzantine geometric, parcel mosaic. **See *opus romanum.***

COSMATI or **COSMATESQUE ARTISTS** Several families were responsible during the 12th and 13th centuries for a geometric mosaic tile decoration using marble fashioned into squares, discs, rectangles, triangles and other shapes to decorate architectural surfaces, namely large-scale floors and walls. The words 'Cosmati' and 'Cosmatesque' derive from the Cosma family who did outstanding work in Rome at that time, and are now used to refer to the artists collectively. In England the best-known example and only true Cosmati floor made by Roman artists with Roman materials is the pavement of London's Westminster Abbey, 1268, the work of Pietro Oderisio (Petrus Odericius).

COW GUM A rubber cement or inert latex-based adhesive used for mounting drawings, etc.

CRAFT KNIVES/STANLEY KNIVES Indispensable retractable and/or reversible knives for scoring, cutting, etc.

CRAFT / KRAFT PAPER Strong brown paper, used in the indirect techniques of mosaic making. It can also be obtained ready-gummed, usually in squared sheets approx. $30cm^2$/ $12in^2$.

CRATER A wide-mouthed bowl for mixing wine and water, used extensively as a decorative motif in Greek and Roman times, for example in many of the large floor mosaics of El Djem in Tunisia (3rd/4th century).

CRENELLATION A motif imitating a fortification wall and used frequently in Classical borders of pavements.

Cosmatesque
The cloister of Monreale (detail of the *chiostrino* or small cloister), late 12th century Sicily, Italy. (EMG)

The cloister comprises 228 paired (geminated) columns around a perfectly square courtyard. Each column has vertical grooves on its shaft carved in arabesques or inset with polychrome / geometric mosaic of various designs in gold and marble – fluted, ophidian (snake-like), wreathed and turned. The exquisite nature of the cosmatesque on a fusion of Arabic, Byzantine and Norman architecture has to be seen to be believed and thereafter never forgotten.

CRUSTA Irregular fragments of limestone or marble, often coloured, and set into a mortar pavement. The term may also refer to slabs of marble used for a wall veneer. **See *chip pavement.***

CUBES Another term that has been used for tesserae, the building units of mosaic making. **See *dice.***

CUBICULUM A bedroom in a Roman dwelling.

CUENCA (Sp. bowl or dish) A technique used in 16th-century Seville, the forerunner of 19th-century dust-pressed imitations, whereby moulds were pressed into the tile surface to form hollow impressions. The term also refers to larger tiles, which had a grid of ridges and were pressed into the surface of the mould when still damp to give the impression of smaller tiles, creating a mosaic-effect tile surface.

CUERDA SECA (Sp. dry cord) A black outline (the 'dry cord') used to separate the colour glazes in tile making. Known of in Moorish times, the device was revived in the 19th century. The outlines were of wax, thinned with spirit and powdered manganese, and were painted on to the surface; the infill colour glazes, often of brilliant colour, shrank away from the wax resist during the firing and the manganese remained as the black outline, giving a mosaic-like illusion.

CULLET Raw or broken waste glass that can be re-melted and re-used; e.g. scrap glass for recycling. In mosaic, the term is used for waste glass or scraps surplus to the smalti-making process but intriguing to the artist.

CUPID See *Eros.*

Cube

Hiatus I, 2001 by Elaine M Goodwin, 97cm x 77cm / 38in x 30in, Venetian gold smalti, mirror mosaic, mirror, ceramic, smalti and marble. (Collection of the University of Exeter) (JM)

The horizontal nature of the work – which, for the artist, signifies infinity – is concentrated in the inner section where the interest is emphasized. The two outer areas composed of regularly cut cubes of Carrara marble help stabilize the image, and the eye, if it wanders, is returned and held on the central area.

CURING This is the term for the chemical process that occurs when a cement and sand mix has water added to it and a hardening process is set in motion. This should be a gradual and natural process, not 'aided' by applying heat, which may occasion cracking. Since shrinkage occurs naturally while drying, the slower and moister the conditions, the better. Where possible cover the concrete with damp cloths or newspaper or cover with plastic sheeting for up to three or four days. The following table can be used as a rough guide in normal (moist) cement-curing conditions:

Portland cement	10 hours setting time	3 days to harden	21 days to cure
Rapid cements	10 hours setting time	24 hours to harden	7 days to cure
Aluminous cements e.g. ciment fondu	3 hours setting time	7 hours to harden	24 hours to cure

CUT-'N'-SNAPS A hard plastic tool for scoring and 'snapping' mosaic tiles; often used for cutting square tesserae diagonally in half.

CUTTERS See *mosaic cutters.*

CUTTERS

Cut shapes using hand-held cutters

| A | B | C | D | E |

C = Is the common tesserae size used.

D = These are used as a running line or to outline forms.

E = These are used in miniature work or areas of great detail.

Cutting in thirds gives alternative sizes

To cut a circle

First cut off the four corners. Then carefully 'nibble' the edges to form a smooth circular shape.

The above shapes are the most commonly used, and can be cut from manufactured vitreous glass and ceramic mosaic tiles (see nibbling).

DABBER A pad made of cloths or rags used instead of a brush to apply a slurry of mortar to a rendered surface before applying the final cement layer to take the mosaic design. I first encountered this excellent way of applying slurry when I worked at the Rock Garden of Sri Nek Chand Saini in India in the 1980s.

DECORATIVE MOSAIC A style of mosaic that gives greatest attention to ornamental or stylistic motifs.

DECUMANUS MAXIMUS The main street lengthways ↕ of a Roman city.

DEESIS 'Entreaty' or prayer of intercession. In Christian mosaics it is a composition showing Christ, flanked by the Mother of God and John the Baptist who are turned towards him, as the central figure, with gestures of intercession.

DELFTWARE Dutch and English decorative ware with an opaque tin glaze on which the design, a landscape or figure, is painted, often in blue.

DENTAL TOOLS Indispensable implements made of steel for probing, picking up and positioning the tesserae when making a mosaic.

DENTILS A tooth-like decorative feature used in border patterns, particularly popular during Roman times.

DESIGN A composition, arrangement or plan, made in preparation for making a mosaic. **See *accent; composition.***

Dabber
The Rock Garden with Nek Chand Saini – detail, 2000, Chandigarh, India. (EMG)

During the 1950s Indian visionary and artist Nek Chand Saini (b. c. 1924) began work on realizing his dream – a sculptural kingdom peopled by all manner of his countrymen and women and animals and depicted in every aspect of their lives. All was to be created in secret, on flat ground, and in recycled materials, particularly chinaware, using concrete as a base. It is a remarkable feat. Now nearing completion and almost 30 hectares in size, it is the second most visited site (after the Taj Mahal) in India. The detail shows Nek Chand looking out from the terrace of the palace constructions, with the architect Le Corbusier's Secretariat and Sculpture in the distance. That two such masters live alongside each other through their work continues the wonderful paradox that is India.

DESIGN ELEMENTS These include line, shape, size, value, colour (contrasts, etc.), direction and texture. When designing for a mosaic, think of 'visual weight' as a key element in the design that will hold the attention. It is an element to be aware of when balancing the design. 'Tension' is a visual regard for the dynamic relationships between parts of the drawing. 'Balance' is a symmetrical/ asymmetrical sense or feel about a centre. 'Formal' areas are those which are of an equal importance and that are visually pleasing. 'Foliated' is a decorative design element or central motif with leaves or curves or lobed foils. See *arabesques; decorative mosaic; ornamental composition.*

Design elements
Mosaic Mural – 1972, watercolour, Hans Unger, Brasenose College, Oxford, England. (JM)

The German-born artist Hans Unger (1915–75) and his friend and assistant Eberhard Schulze were in the forefront of mosaic making in the 1960s and 1970s in England. Unger's thorough understanding of mosaic as an art form in its own right, independent of painting and sculpture, has influenced present-day artists through his work and writings. This watercolour for a mosaic mural for an Oxford college uses the polyhedron, a medieval symbol of research, as its focal point, in a mosaic design which uses line, 'optical play' and spatial values to create a strong composition.

DEVITRIFICATION A process in which glass becomes somewhat crystallized, either as it cools from the molten state (too slow!), or as a result of an unstable composition or firing.

DIAMOND SAW A tool with a cutting edge used for cutting tiles or slate. A diamond abrasive pad may be used afterwards for smoothing rough edges on glass or ceramic tesserae.

DICE Another (now rarely used) term for tesserae. See *cubes.*

DIE (1) A tessera; (2) a metal or plaster of Paris plate placed on the top and bottom of a tile when pressed.

DIRECT METHOD (It. *metodo diretto*) One of the most popular methods of laying a mosaic, as the surface of the work can be seen at all times throughout its making. General procedure: apply an appropriate adhesive, either on each individual tessera, or by covering an area over a suitable base material (wood, concrete, netting, metal, etc.) and then set out the individual tesserae to build up a mosaic. For example, if using the direct method on to fibre netting (It. *mosaico su rete in fibra di vetro*): draw the design on paper (if very large cut this into sections). Cut the fibre netting/mesh to fit over each section. Place a sheet of polythene between the drawing and the netting, so that the drawing is visible and the adhesive is prevented from sticking to the paper. Fix the mosaic tesserae for the design

Direct method
Profeta, 2000 by Stefano Mazzotti, 110cm x 110cm / 44 x 44in, smalti, gold and natural stones.

Stefano Mazzotti (b. 1951) is an Italian artist who was born and continues to live, in Ravenna, Italy, where he studied at the Accademia di Belle Arti. His work, often symbolic, mysterious and intimate, reveals similar qualities to the mosaic masters of Byzantium that surround him in the basilicas of his city. He works directly on to wood, allowing his chosen materials space to work both with and against each other.

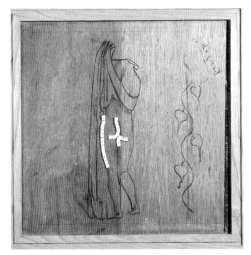

A.

B.

C.

directly on to the netting. Tesserae may be of any size and shape, placed flat or angled. When the whole is completed, allow to dry, then lift and attach to the permanent surface; grout or not as needed. *Advantages of the above technique*: (1) small or large scale mosaics can be fixed to any surface, both internally and externally, without a pre-cut backing board or support; (2) angling of pieces is maintained to give a freer artistic expression. *Disadvantages*: very large or heavy tesserae or fragile and vertical pieces fixed to the work are difficult to transport, as the netting is somewhat flexible and repositioning or transporting of the work could therefore be precarious. **See** *'laying'*.

Direct method

A Muse Turns, 2003 by Elaine M Goodwin, 66cm x 66cm / 26in x 26in, Carrara marble, Venetian gold, smalti. (Private collection.) (JM)

A. The drawing is made directly on to a timber base board and 'firmed up' with a permanent marker pen to dispense with any 'feathery' under-drawing. The base is then primed with a colourless adhesive. Small cubes of white Carrara marble are cut on the hammer and hardie and set on the base to outline the main lines of the figure.

B. They are then fixed directly into a cement adhesive and as the cement sets, any surplus adhesive is scraped away with a palette knife to allow a fairly tight tessellation. White smalti are then cut and used for the drapery at the side and across the figure, to make only a very slight, if important, interplay between the similar coloured materials – one of the author's characteristic juxtapositions.

C. The 'attribute' of the Muse is also made of white smalti, and then the background of gold, using Opus Palladianum, begins to surround the figure, each tessera being pressed into a cement adhesive bed to give a gently undulating surface to diffuse the light.

D. The muse is often identified as an inspiring power, one that no artist can live without. This work by the author singles out the character of the muse – its arbitrary and capricious nature. Entitled 'A Muse Turns', it immediately invokes ambiguity: to turn away? or to turn toward? This uncertainty is ever present in the artist's mind – what might on one occasion appear playful, direct and inspired thought, another time may seem wayward and distant.

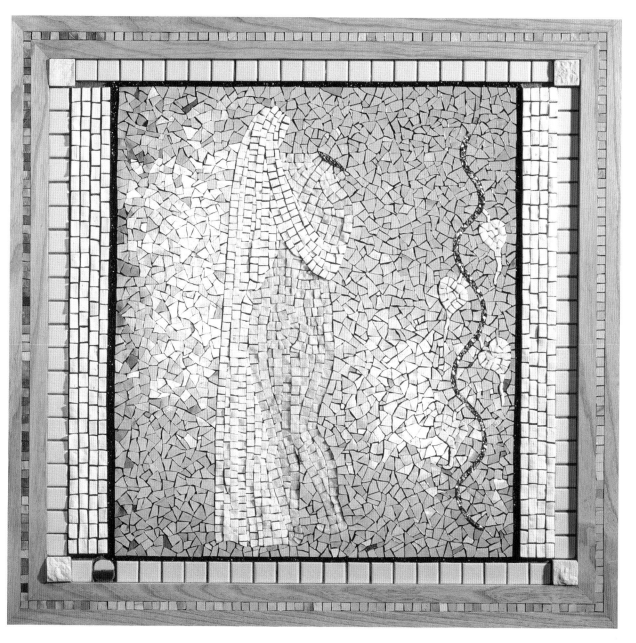

D.

DIRECTIONAL LINES See *andamento; flow.*

DIVISIONISM A mosaic technique using optical mixing, involving the placing of individual colours together and viewing them at a distance. For example, where there is an area of similar colours made up of different materials this may be enhanced by interspersing harmonies, as in large areas of purple where red and blue tesserae can be dropped in as an enlivening optical mix. **See *juxtaposition; pointillism.***

DOMUS A Roman town house, the villa being more specifically a country house.

DOUBLE REVERSE METHOD (also 'reciprocal' method) This is a method that can be used to overcome the 'sameness' sometimes achieved in the indirect method, and which at the same time gives flexibility of choice of fixing position. It is generally only used for small-scale works. The tesserae are positioned in a bed of moist fine-grained sand, contained in a frame or box. They may be set at angles and to different depths. Soak one or two layers of fine muslin (cheesecloth) in a waterbased adhesive and carefully mould them on to the surface of the mosaic. Allow them to dry completely. The mosaic can then be lifted and placed in a fresh mortar bed – this may be on a ceiling, a dome or a wall. When set permanently, the muslin is soaked with hot water and eased carefully off the tiles. There will be no need to grout unless necessary.

DRILL A hole-forming tool, turned by hand, foot or electricity. It is used for drilling wood and hard stone or masonry, in which latter case masonry bits or iron points are substituted.

DUST CLAY This is a prepared clay, dried and finely ground, to which water has been gently added. It was used in tile presses from the 19th century.

DYNAMIC This refers to the energy or directional movement of the tesserae within a mosaic.

EASEL MOSAIC A generic name for a mosaic when it is not part of an architectural element, e.g. a wall or floor. Today many such mosaics are designed and made by the mosaic artist, often being original and very much at the forefront of modern mosaic-making. **See *portable/portative icon*.**

EDGING-BAND The plain strip of mosaic floor around the circumference of a room outside the main decorated area of mosaic. In Classical mosaics this is frequently composed of distinctly larger, more crudely cut tesserae.

EGYPT From the earliest dynasties of ancient Pharaonic Egypt examples of mosaic decoration have been found on columns and capitals, decorating palaces and temples. Small domestic objects were also inlaid with minute pieces of glass and semiprecious stones, examples of which can be seen in the Cairo Museum, Egypt.

EGYPTIAN BLUE (also known as blue frit: $CaOCuO_4SiO_2$) A blue pigment used in shell mosaics of the late 1st century BC. According to Vitruvius, it was imported from Egypt and later

Easel mosaic
Elaine, 1970s by Arthur Goodwin, 64cm x 79cm / 25in x 31in, unglazed ceramic, smalti. (JM)

This is a portrait of the author by the English artist Arthur Goodwin, born in Ormskirk, Liverpool (1922–98). The artist was a painter, writer, teacher and mosaic artist, and it was under his tutelage at Exeter College of Art in England that the author became aware of the art of mosaic. The portrait uses simple, unglazed ceramic tiles and was carried out as a painting, i.e. vertically on an easel with the tesserae pressed into the mastic. Note the contrast between the painterly treatment of the face and the regular opus tessellatum of the overshirt.

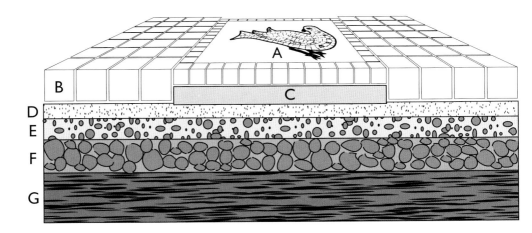

This diagram illustrates the placing of an emblema, and shows the cross section of a classical pavement foundation according to Vitruvius.

A Mosaic emblema, made of finer tesserae.

B Mosaic surround, made of larger tesserae.

C Tray on which the emblema is made.

D Fine setting bed, nucleus.

E Coarse layer of mortar and aggregate, rudus.

F Layer of rubble, well tamped down, statumen.

G Earth.

made in Italy at Puteoli. It is believed to have been the only synthetic colour in antiquity. It was made by heating together silica, malachite, calcium carbonate (chalk) and natron; this was made into a paste, then fired at approx. 850ºC and rolled into pellets 6mm to 12mm (^{1}/4 in to ^{1}/2 in) long. These were first thought to have been used in mosaics of the 1st century BC in Leptis Magna (North Africa) and in Pompeii (Italy, before AD 79). Jars of these pellets have been found in a Roman shipwreck off Malta.

EMBLEMA / Gk. EMBΛHMA (pl. **emblemata**, an inset / insets) A central, usually figurative, panel inserted into a floor in Greek and Roman mosaics. It was often prepared in fine mosaic away from site in stone or marble trays or travertine plate; e.g. Nilotic Scene, House of the Menander, Pompeii, Italy (before AD 79). Further superb examples from Pompeii and Herculaneum can be seen in the Archaeological Museum, Naples, Italy. The terms 'false emblema' and 'pseudo emblema' are also used to mean a central panel that was made at site and not therefore detachable.

EMERY PAPER / wet-dry paper A paper of various granular textures, dust or powders. It is often used as a substitute for carborundum and also as a cleaning agent to clean or grind surface deposits of cement from a mosaic. It can also be used as an aid when cutting and smoothing hard stones. **See *grinder.***

ENAMEL (Fr. *émail*) The vitreous glaze applied to a surface of glass or ceramic, which is then fired. Venetian smalti are often incorrectly termed Venetian enamel.

ENAMELLING From c. 400 BC, inlays of glassy appearance were used in decorative designs, at first in red, then blue and yellow; examples can be seen on shields, harnesses etc., and from 1st century AD on brooches. It can be found as a vitreous substance fused to a metallic base, mostly bronze. Early usage, alongside shells and marble, is to be seen at the Villa of Horace in Tivoli, Rome, Italy.

ENCAUSTIC TILE A tile whose design is 'let into' it, and is not just surface decoration.

ENGRAVING A technique of cutting into the surface of glass.

EPOXY GROUT A two-part waterproof grout, used in kitchen areas or where hygiene is paramount. **See *grout/grouting.***

EPOXY RESINS / GLASS PLASTICS Non-soluble synthetic resins are used as very strong and efficient adhesives. They are highly resistant to temperature and chemicals. Sand and pigment can be added for strength and colour. Epoxy resin is an excellent adhesive for bonding non-porous glass to glass; when set it is permanent and waterproof. It is a two-component adhesive (resin + hardener). Once mixed, the two components release heat by an internal chemical reaction that cannot be reversed;

Epoxy resin
Pensiero à Michelangelo, 2002 by Felice Nittolo, 131.5cm x 125.5cm x 12cm / 52in x 49in x 5in, marble, smalti, Venetian gold, shells, plaster, metal.

The Italian artist, Felice Nittolo was born in 1950 in Irpinia and trained at the Istituto d'Arte in Avellino and at the Accademia di Belle Arte in Naples. He has for many years made his home and studios in Ravenna, Italy, where he is a master teacher at the Istituto Statale d'Arte 'Gino Severini'. A prolific and experimental artist, Nittolo explores the mosaic medium in 3D and 2D mosaic, occasionally collaborating his visual works with music, theatre and poetry. This work, a direct setting of marble into resin, undermines its controlled composure with a sense of imminent disturbance.

the mixture will become extremely hard and solid. Its hardening time depends on the surrounding temperature; a warmer temperature hastens the process.

Application: use equal proportions, mix well, and apply to grease-free, dry surfaces. Bring together and either hold, clamp or press till set. When using resins always work in a well-ventilated area and wear adequate protective clothing. To create a resin base: make up the mosaic on paper. Prepare a mould or containing frame and use paper or a wax parting agent to prevent the resin sticking to its inner surface. Place a layer of woven glass fibre over the mosaic and of the exact size. Mix up the resin + curing agent (when using large quantities place in a plastic bowl), and pour it over the glass fibre to a depth of approx. 4mm / $^1/_8$ in and allow to set. It might be necessary to use two or three layers of fibre. Leave to cure, or until the 'tacky' quality has gone. Carefully release the mosaic, turn over and remove any paper from the other side and grout as normal and leave to set. Any rough edges can be smoothed. In this way a lightweight backing support is made for the mosaic.

EROS (pl. **erotes**) In mosaic Eros (Greek) or Cupid (Roman) is depicted as a winged youth signifying Love personified. A lovely example of two erotes or winged children (also known as *amorini* in Italian) accompany their Mother Venus in the so-called Low Ham mosaic (4th century) in Taunton Museum, England. It was originally made for a *frigidarium* of a villa.

ETIMASIA 'Preparation'. A Christian iconographic motif on Byzantine mosaic shown as an empty throne with a cross above it; signifying the getting ready for the return and judgement of Christ, e.g. S. Prassede, Rome, Italy, 9th century.

EXEDRA An open-air, open-fronted area, often with a semicircular apse, used for meetings and for conversation.

EXPANDED METAL MESH See *aluminium mesh.*

EYE SHIELDS (goggles) It is imperative to wear eye protection when operating machinery, e.g. grinders, band saws; or when cutting mosaic materials for tesserae. **See** *safety.*

FAIENCE Pottery to which a glazed siliceous paste, blue or green, of Egyptian origin, has been applied. It is now understood to be earthenware covered with lead tin glaze designs. A popular production place during the Renaissance was Faenza in Italy (hence the name), and its popularity spread, especially in France where it continues to be enjoyed.

FAUCES An entrance passage in a traditional Roman house.

FEATHER MOSAIC See *Mexican mosaic.*

FELSPAR/FELDSPAR A field crystal that is easily cleavable or cut. It is found in granite, usually white, pink or creamy yellow, and is not affected by acid.

FELT-TIP PENS / MARKERS These are useful pens for designing, sketching and drawing. They may be permanent or not.

FIBREGLASS When polyester resin and glass fibre are combined they produce a material that is both lightweight and very strong.

Fibreglass Procedure

1 Pour laminating resin into a plastic bowl and add the recommended amount of liquid hardener

2 Add smallish pieces of glass fibre and mix with the resin mixture

3 Add an inert filler powder (this may be marble dust, slate filler, graphite powder or a metal filler – these are obtained as bronze, iron, copper, brass or nickel particles)

4 Knead (using barrier cream or rubber gloves)

5 Apply to an expanded metal support or into the mould

6 Counteract any stickiness by adding more of the filler powder

7 Press the tesserae into the mixture. This mixture can be 'worked' for about 30–40 minutes; it is therefore better to use small quantities at a time in a well-ventilated area to produce a virtually indestructible and portable 2D or 3D base.
See ***glass fibre.***

FIGLINUM See *opus figlinum.*

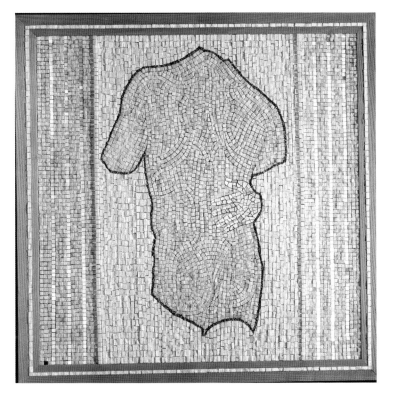

Figurative
Ecce Homo, 2002 by Elaine M Goodwin, 114cm x 114cm / 45in x 45in, Carrara marble, smalti, Venetian gold, antique gold. (Private collection.) (JM)

The author studied in England at Exeter College of Art and Design (in the 1970s) where she worked with 3D form in plaster, often involving the figure. Mosaic for her is a medium of reduction – a honing down of concept or, in this case, the male form, to its essentials. The work has tenuous links with Titian's painting of the same title.

FIGURATIVE MOSAIC 'Representational', often using the human figure in part or in whole.

FILATO (pl. **filati**; rod / rods) A single tessera of glass smalti or lump of glass paste, often of a master tint – i.e. of very concentrated colour – is heated over a flame and stretched between tweezers to form a long thread or *filato*. When cold this is cut into tiny circular tesserae and the cut ends used in miniature mosaics. Also referred to as threads, rods and spun canes.

FIN (or flash) A projection of concrete or cement mix that protrudes from between the tesserae, e.g. in the indirect method, after concrete is poured into a frame or mould. If left too long before turning over to reveal the surface, small fins of concrete may have seeped through the backing material. These may be dispensed with, using a chisel and hammer.

FINISH Occasionally a mosaic after completion needs finishing touches. For glass use a silicone wax polish. For marble, first warm the marble and use an equal mix of warmed beeswax and turpentine. Make up small quantities. While both are still warm rub into the marble with a soft rag. Then buff the marble, taking care not to let the wax congeal. Other means of finishing include filling, grinding, sanding and smoothing using glass paper or sandpaper. **See *carborundum; grinding wheel.***

FITCH A brush made of stiff hog hair, ideal for brushing away glass debris from the worktable.

FLEXIBLE BONDING The result achieved by the use of cement-based adhesives or latex adhesives which, when mixed, have more elasticity and a good vertical grip/slip. They give more latitude of movement for exterior mosaics in situations where normal bonding would be too rigid and encourage cracks in the grouting. Where there is need for some 'give' in laying mosaics for walls or floors, e.g. on wooden floorboards, use proprietary brands with latex or a cement-based flexi-adhesive, and grout with a flexi-grout. **See *cement-based adhesives; grout.***

FLINT A brittle mineral stone of silica, often straw yellow in colour.

FLOAT A tool used for grouting: it has rounded corners and bevelled edges, and is usually rubber-faced. It is used for spreading and pushing grout across the mosaic surface. **See *notched trowel.***

FLOOR (foundation) To make a mosaic floor a sound foundation is essential. It generally consists of three layers to form a thick concrete

---

Floor Procedure

1 Dig deep – 30cm to 50cm / 12in to 20in

2 Add up to 20cm / 8in of coarse rubble (Classical: statumen) – this could be stones, brick or gravel – and pound or ram it down to give good drainage.

3 Make and add a mortar made with aggregate or gravel (classical: rudus) up to approx. 20cm / 8in. Roughen up the surface or score it with a trowel to make a key for the next layer.

4 Make and add a smooth cement/sand mortar as a foundation cement (Classical: nucleus).

5 Lay mosaic, either directly, indirectly or both. Remember to moisten the surface before laying the mosaic if traditional cement mortar is used to embed the mosaic. Leave the surface dry if a cement adhesive is preferred. (See diagram, p. 52.)

Figurative
Scultura Vivente, 2000 by Felice Nittolo; dimensions – natural!, marble, smalti and gold.

The Ravenese artist Felice Nittolo is an experimenter par excellence in mosaic. Here, at the Arte Fiera (Art Fair) in Bologna, Italy in 2000, at a performance of Scultura Vivente he models his own work, becoming a living mosaic sculpture. The coat was made on a black pigmented silicon resin base using flexible netting. Often provocative, Nittolo has for 30 years been pushing the boundaries of the mosaic medium.

bed, with a good surface for receiving the mosaic, as so soundly stated by Vitruvius and Pliny, who had a secure knowledge of the principles of floormaking.

FLORENTINE MOSAIC / *pietre dure* (lit. 'hard stones') A technique prevalent in Florence, Italy, at the end of the 16th century, which is still being used today. Semiprecious stones and marble are cut into thin layers, given shapes and fixed together, apparently seamlessly. The intrinsic patterns and highlights in the materials are used to maximum effect. It arose from *opus sectile* (which is effectively marquetry) in the ancient Roman world. Any technique that denies the interstices or grout gaps is not mosaic in the true sense and as I understand it! **See** *pietre dure.*

FLOUR AND WATER PASTE A cheap and effective temporary paste for the indirect method of mosaic making. Procedure: mix 1 part flour with 8 parts water, and stir and boil for 5 minutes. Strain. Use for reverse mosaic making. When dry, remove any paper backing with warm water.

Flow
Path, nos 7 and 9 (details of two of 12 individual panels), 2001 by Sonia King, 23cm x 53cm / 9in x 21in (complete mosaic 2.76m x 6.36m / 108in x 252in minimum), ceramic, glass, marble, shell, Venetian gold, smalti.

The American mosaicist Sonia King uses the medium of mosaic as a map, an exploration of the medium through concepts combined with a sense of place. In these two details the tesserae are 'taken for a walk' as each panel is linked through both real and imagined movement.

FLOW The apparent movement created by placing tesserae in a continuous direction, following a form or contour. This can be varied to give dynamic to the mosaic, and is a very important element for imparting life and interest. Sometimes it is advisable to indicate the 'movement' in a cartoon and to be aware of it when creating a work. **See _andamento._**

FONDO (pl. **fondi**) **D'ORO** The base of a vessel incorporating a gold foil decoration

FORICA A Roman latrine. There is a lively mosaic fragment in the loo at Piazza Armerina in Sicily, 4/5th century AD.

FORNACIAIO (furnace-man) The term for a glassmaker.

FOUNDATION CEMENT The cement used as a base to fix tesserae into. This is usually smooth and can be coloured if the mosaic is to be ungrouted.

FRACTURING FEEL When tesserae are cut with hand nippers, each material and each colour cuts

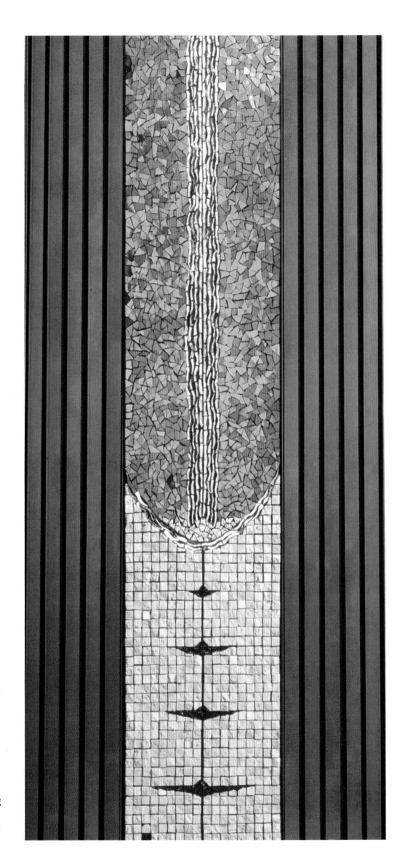

Framing

That's Me, 2002 by Elaine M Goodwin, 36cm x 80cm /
14in x 32in ,Venetian copper gold, silvered glass,
marble, metal frame. (Artist's collection; frame Mike
Helman.) (JM)

In this mosaic by the author, one of a pair, the frame
was made integral to the work as a whole. The
narrow side strips were made to emphasize the
vertical nature of the work. For the artist the framing
of her work – if there at all! – has an inherent role to
play; it may be simply structural, protective or part of
the whole concept.

with a noticeably different pressure. For example, in vitreous glass, the black or terracotta-coloured glass tesserae are notoriously brittle as opposed to ordinary more 'sandy' vitreous glass colours of blue or green, which need little effort to cut. As artists familiarize themselves with cutting, allowances and variants of pressure are given to each cut automatically.

FRAMING A frame should be used only to contain or complement the work. It may be made in any width in (a) wood; (b) metal, e.g. strips/lengths of aluminium, copper, brass etc. or (c) tesserae or tiles. Do not frame if a sense of continuation into space is needed – seal the edges with adhesive, cement or other.

FRESCO A type of mural painting using lime-proof pigments that are applied to fresh lime plaster and become permanent when dry.

FRIGIDARIUM A room in a Roman bath house or *thermae* that has cold-water pools.

FROSTING A network of small cracks on the surface of glass or glazed tiles that may be caused by cold temperatures. Be aware of this when using tiles for external work in countries where frosts and freezing temperatures are likely to occur.

Framing
Aspiration for Penetration, 1994 by George Trak, 2.4m x 1.3m / 94in x 51in, marble, stainless steel.

The Bulgarian artist George Trak (b. 1961 in Plovdiv, Bulgaria) studied at the Fine Art Academy in Sofia from 1985 to 1990. He continues to live and work in the city of his birth. Prolific and innovative, the artist exploits strength and energy in all his work, whether working with watercolours, oil paintings, glass assemblage or in particular mosaic. Much of his work in mosaic is three-dimensional, the natural qualities of granite and marble appearing soft within twisting or hard-edged steel frames.

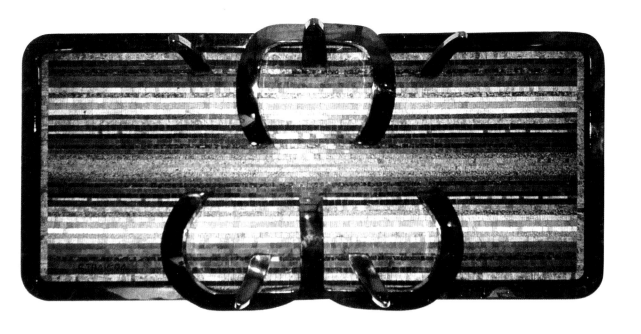

G

GALVANIZED METAL / WIRE A form of rust-resistant treatment for wire and metal (such as chicken wire mesh or even metal coat hangers), that can be used for reinforcement of concrete, or for building up on an armature as a support base for a three-dimensional structure.

GAMMA The Greek letter Γ.

GAMMADION (pl. **gammadia,** lit. 'a small gamma') The monogram seen on the cloaks of mosaic figures from the 2nd century AD (Roman) to the 13th century. They originated in Palestine as a form of decoration made by the cloth weavers. See e.g. S. Apollinare Nuovo (6th century AD) and San Vitale (6th century AD) in Ravenna, Italy, the church of Angeloktistos ('built by angels') (6th century AD) near Kyrenia in Cyprus, and St Maria Maggiore (13th century) in Rome, Italy. The designs are thought to have begun as calligraphic ornament, as initials often using Roman letters, e.g. P (Peter); H (JoHannes), I (Jesus). **See** *tablion.*

GAUZE FABRIC (1) In conservation work, one or two layers of this loosely woven fabric can be glued (often using Primal AC33) on to the surface of a mosaic to aid lifting or repositioning. (2) Gauze or muslin (cheesecloth) is also used soaked in cement slurry to build up forms over an armature. It is also used to clean mosaic after grouting. **See** *hessian; scrim.*

GENRE MOSAIC A mosaic having representations of everyday life (i.e. not myth or history).

GEOMETRIC TILE PAVEMENTS Floors made up of plain tiles of various geometric shapes and colours arranged in geometric configurations. The motifs are many, ranging from simple chequer-board patterns to complex multipatterned compositions. **See** *guilloche; cable pattern; lozenge; meander.*

GESSO A gypsum or chalk bound with size or fish glue and used as a ground on which to paint.

GIALLO ANTICO (lit. 'old yellow') A Numidian marble from Simitthus (Chemtou) in Africa. It is a yellow colour with occasional red veining.

GILBERT COLLECTION Arthur and Rosalinde Gilbert were collectors of post-Renaissance Italian mosaics and other fine art objects. These were assembled from the late 1960s and later given as a collection to London UK, where they can be viewed by the public.

GIORNATA A day's work. For example, on the final plaster layer on a wall, up to about 1 m² / 1 yd² may be achieved depending on the intricacy of the design and the materials used. Changes in plaster colour can be seen in some Byzantine mosaics, where daily mortar mixes have differed. This makes the making of the ancient mosaic seem very immediate and human.

GLASS A homogeneous, inorganic and extremely durable material even in humid and hot, dry conditions. Glassware was made from at least 2500 BC; and glass objects, e.g. beads, are known from 3000 BC. During late Augustan and Tiberian times glass was used more in mosaics; at first from broken glass vessels, glass disks and twisted glass rods. Glass factories were established in Italy under Augustus. One of earliest buildings to use glass tesserae as true mosaic on a wall was the *columbarium* (communal tomb) of Pomponius Hylas at Rome, Italy, early 1st century AD, which combines cockle shells and twisted glass rods, as well as making limited use of green, yellow and blue glass, and blue frit. From this

Gauze fabric
Monastery of Daphni, Attica, Greece, 11/12th century, detail, Archangel. (EMG)

The monastery of Daphni has mosaics in the dome, squinches, esonarthex and sanctuary. The images are from the life of Christ and the Virgin Mary. They are captivating. Sadly, many of the mosaics have been damaged by earthquakes but are being repaired under the expert guidance of Dimitrios Chrysopoulos. In this detail the gauze is protecting the surface of the tesserae while fresh mortars are applied to re-secure their placement. Note, too, how a sheet of clear polythene covering part of the angel is used to record the exact positioning of each tessera for reference during conservation.

time onwards, cut glass tesserae were used as their values became well understood, including their ability to catch light and add sparkle as a background to water (e.g. in nymphaea).

Glass can be transparent, translucent, opalescent, opaque, colourless or coloured. It can be shaped when heated by moulding, blowing, casting, or pressing. It can be textured or decorated with enamel or paint, used as appliqué, or with the addition of metal leaf. It comes in at about 6 on the hardness scale (**see** *Mohs scale*). Glass was used in Romano-British mosaics for adding colour and highlighting, and was often incorporated into mosaics using glass fragments from broken vessels; e.g. red on the flowers of the head-dress of Spring in the Seasons mosaic, Cirencester (Corinium), late 2nd century AD, and green on the tails of the two birds at the Roman villa at Bignor, Sussex, c. 4th century AD.

GLASS BEVELS Pre-shaped faceted glass shapes, e.g. diamond, circular, oval, star and triangle used in stained-glass making and mosaic work. **See** *bevel*.

GLASS CUTTERS Tools for cutting glass and mirror. The simplest forms have steel cutting wheels, often of tungsten carbide while others have self-lubricating wheels using an oil reservoir. Circular glass cutters are good for cutting both mirror and all types of glass. For general cutting, hold the cutting wheel perpendicular to the surface of the glass or mirror and apply firm downward pressure – it gives off a scratching sound. Lift the scored glass in each hand and twist outwards between thumbs and forefingers, and use the ball end of the cutter to tap along the underside of the scoreline before twisting outwards. Never score the line repeatedly – once only!

GLASS FIBRE This is made from filaments of glass and used to reinforce polyester resin; it is also used in netting to form a reinforcing mesh for resin, resulting in a strong, light, tough material. **See** *armature; ciment fondu; fibreglass.*

GLASS FIBRE MESH This is glass fibre manufactured into a variety of forms. It is used for reinforcement, and in levelling screeds. It is resistant to alkalis (e.g. cement mortars), and gives good light backing support. There are different types of glass fibre; use fine 5cm / 2in ribbon for edge reinforcement, and for 3D work use chopped strand mat, available in sheets that can be cut for building up. It is commonly used dipped in a cement slurry and applied to an armature. Wear gloves to press it on to the support base and ensure thorough coverage. It is also referred to as netting; fibre netting; mesh. **See** *direct method*.

GLASS PAPER This is used for smoothing and finishing rough areas of wood after cutting. It is also referred to as sandpaper or garnet paper.

GLASS PASTE TESSERAE In mosaic this term is used for tesserae that are traditional and practically lead-free (less than 5% lead oxide). High lead tesserae (5% to 60%) are very brilliant because of a high refraction index, and are easier to cut (softer). The qualities of glass paste tesserae were noted early on; they were lightweight and imparted good vertical adhesion to plaster as well as being more impermeable to weather than stone and marble. Their refracted surfaces, when used in nymphaea, rebounded light on to water and enriched the effects of colour. Very early use of glass paste tesserae can be found in mosaics of the late 2nd and early 1st century BC, *in situ* in the archaeological site of the

Glass cutters

(Left)
Photograph showing how to hold and use a simple single-wheel glass cutter. The glass is scored towards the artist for straight lines, and away for curves. Always keep the cutter vertical to the glass. Use an even pressure to produce a thin silvery line on the glass, and oil the wheel from time to time. (JM)

(Right)
Photograph showing a glass cutting tool with a built-in oil reservoir for smooth lubrication, which is very useful if cutting from a large sheet of mirror or glass into myriad tesserae. Hold the cutter like a pencil and again keep an even pressure. (JM)

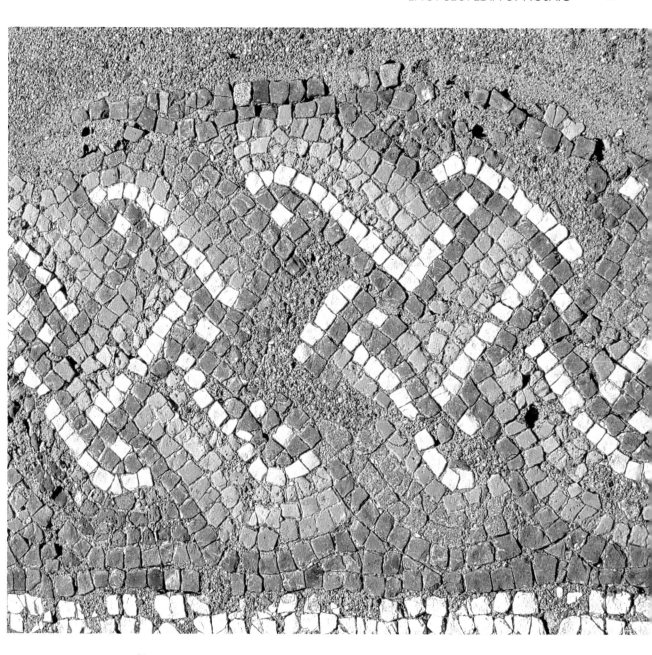

Glass paste tesserae
The Great Baths (*thermae*), detail, showing a guilloche pattern, 2nd/3rd century AD,
Dion, Northern Greece. (EMG)

The archaeological site of Dion, excavated in the early 20th century, lies in the
foothills of Mount Olympus, sacred home of the ancient gods of Greek mythology.
The site has many sanctuaries, a theatre, villas and a great baths complex. There are
a number of floor mosaics to be seen *in situ* and also in a nearby museum. There is
much evidence of the use of colourful glass paste tesserae. This border detail in the
bath area shows strong green and yellow tesserae alongside black, white and
terracotta-coloured marble in a guilloche or braid pattern.

sacred island of Delos. Glass paste tesserae are also found from the first half of the 1st century AD from sites around Vesuvius. In the 1st century AD they are even in texture and colour, and sharply cut; by the 3rd century AD they appear 'bubbly' and cracked and less regular in size. There have been many recent discoveries in Rome, e.g. in vaults of the Baths of Diocletian, where they are approx. 1cm / ¹/₂in in length and very irregular. Early glass tesserae used primary colours; in the 2nd and 3rd centuries, pinks, purples and orange were introduced.

GLASS SHEETS AND GLASS OBJECTS When glass is used as a backing support, glue the tesserae with a clear silicone adhesive and position for maximum light effects.

GLAZE An impervious vitrified final surface that gives a sheen to a tile.

Globs
Starburst Triptych (detail), 2000 by Paul San Casciani, stained-glass, foil-backed globs, crushed glass.

The artist Paul San Casciani, of Italian lineage, was born in London and studied in the 1950s at the esteemed studio of James Powell (Whitefriars, London). He specializes in glass painting, and designing and making stained glass. The triptych is a three-panelled assemblage, inspired by the rich colour usage of the mosaics in Antoni Gaudi's mosaics in Parc Güell in Barcelona, Spain, and uses opalescent and iridescent glass combined with unique handmade glass globs or 'jewels'. The panel, a garden mirror/window incorporates five starbursts, and relies for optimum colour and illusion when seen against an ever-changing background of garden planting.

GLOBS, GLOBULES, NUGGETS, JEWELS Baubles of glass in many colours including iridescent or iridized finishes, used in mosaic and in stained-glass work.

GLUE See *adhesives.*

GNEISS A hard, sparkling crystalline rock of quartz, feldspar and mica.

GOLD Natural gold is almost never without silver! If there is more than 20 per cent silver, it becomes white gold/electrum. Gold is very resilient to corrosion by atmosphere and chemical attacks. The carat represents the amount of alloy, as natural gold is very soft. There is no silver in 24 carat gold, but, for example, in 18 carat gold there are 18 parts gold to six parts silver or copper.

GOLD GLASS First known in the 3rd century BC or even slightly earlier. Early examples from Canosa in Southern Italy show vessels with a layer of gold leaf cut into intricate designs, pressed between an inner and outer layer of transparent glass. This began a tradition of using gold by glass workers from 3rd century BC up to the early 3rd century AD. Subjects included portraits, and later Christian subjects, on the base discs from vessels and on medallions. Sometimes the designs were incised through the gold leaf, which was applied to the glass and covered and protected by a thin glass film. These early techniques of ancient craftsmen are still not yet fully understood by modern scientists and technical experts.

'GOLD' GLASS By using gold, aluminium, copper, etc., leaf, and sticking this to a surface glass with clear adhesive, mosaic practitioners can make 'gold' glass to order. Various types of glass can be used – textured, coloured, riveted or plain. The metal shows through the glass for enhanced and brilliant effect, and the cost is considerably less than the price of the real thing. An alternative is to add an oil gold size on to the surface of the glass and leave it to become tacky. Then gold or silver leaf, etc., is gently pressed on to this for a permanent hold. Tarnishing will occur if metallic leaf is used, but not with gold leaf. **See** *water gilding.*

GOLD LEAF This is very thinly beaten gold of various weights, often 23–24 carat. The colour is in part determined by the purity of the gold.

Gold smalti
Gold roundel, 11.5cm / 7in diameter.

The gold sandwiched between an upper and a base layer of glass is beaten to 0.15 thousandths of a millimetre. Today, one cubic centimetre / approx. 1/2 in of gold yields 6 sq m (over 6 square yards) of gold. The thin glass covering (*cartellina*) on to which the gold was adhered, is attached to a yellow-coloured backing glass, in this case an antique glass, as most gold used today has a turquoise or green backing glass.

GOLD SMALTI (It. *smalto oro*) This is an erroneous term that has come into general use today and is accepted by most practitioners. This material is not genuine smalti, but genuine gold leaf (also silver, aluminium and copper), which is embedded between one normally thinner layer of surface glass which may be smooth, rippled (granulated) or ancient (crazed), and another generally thicker base glass. In this way gold can be used in mosaic protected from atmospheric, weather and temperature changes. The thin surface glass (*cartellina*), up to 1mm / 1/20 in thick, can be coloured (blue, green, pink, etc.) for special effects, and the thicker base glass, 5–7mm / 1/8–1/3in, can be coloured for deeper, lighter or richer effect. By using the material in reverse with the metal shining through the glass, intensely brilliant colour effects can be achieved. A superb if expensive material. It is also called Venetian gold.

Gold smalti
A selection of golden tesserae of various sizes (approx. 0.5cm – 8cm /
^{1}/4 in–3in) cut from roundels, with granulated (rippled) and smooth surfaces. (JM)

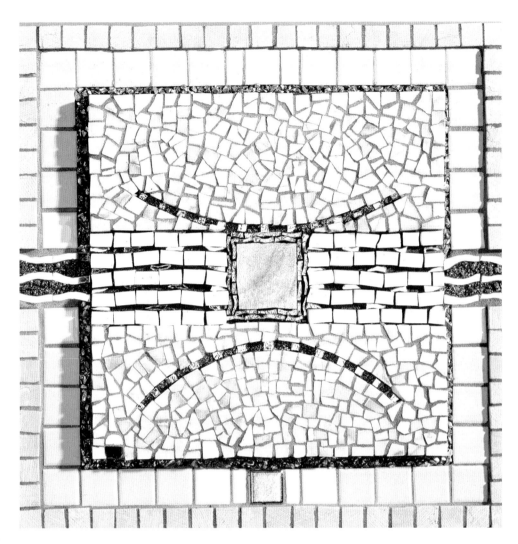

Gold smalti

Serenissima I, 2002 by Elaine M Goodwin, 36cm x 36cm / 14in x 14in, Venetian gold smalti, marble, silvered glass, glazed ceramic, matt ceramic. (JM)

The author is preoccupied with light in her work – an elusive element. Light effects can be 'caught' in the light-reflecting surfaces of glass and metals, which in turn rely on a light source. In this work, the first of a series paying homage to Venice, 'La Serenissima I', she suspends a single antique gold smalti slab for extolment by the surrounding tesserae.

GOLDEN SECTION A 19th-century English name for an idealized proportion in a design, corresponding to Euclid's division of a line, whereby the ratio of the shorter area to the longer area is equal to the longer area's relationship to the whole. It is often the instinctive area of a composition where the interest is most concentrated – possibly a subconscious act by an artist? It is also known as 'divine proportion'.

'GOO' / SLURRY A cement mortar mix with extra water, used as a bonding adhesive between successive layers of cement. **See *slurry.***

GRAECANIUM A Greco–Roman mortar that imparted thermal properties and was employed in winter dining areas (*triclinia*). It was a dark-coloured cement made up of a mix of charcoal, lime, ashes and sand.

Golden section – diagram

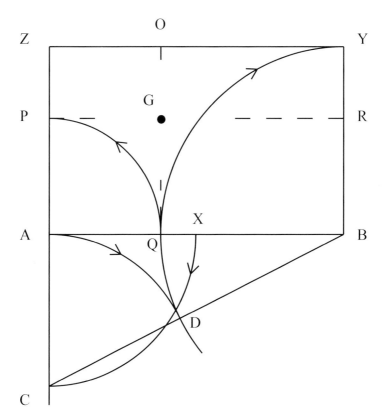

Diagram to determine the centre of interest for a mosaic panel (JM)

1) On a sheet of paper, draw a base line AB of chosen length and mark its centre at X.
2) Drop a perpendicular line from A.
3) Scribe an arc from X to C with A as centre point.
4) Join CB.
5) Scribe an arc from A to D with C as centre point.
6) Scribe an arc from D to Y with B as centre point marking Q on line AB.
7) Draw verticals from A and B and complete rectangle ABYZ.
8) Scribe an arc from Q to P with A as centre point.
9) Draw the co-ordinates PR and QO. These meet at point G which is the Golden Mean.
10) Transfer the drawing to wood, netting, etc.

GRANITE A coarse crystalline rock that can be white, black, grey, green, pink or red, and is made up of quartz, feldspar and mica. A popular natural material for mosaic.

GRAPHITE TRANSFER PAPER A tracing paper used in drawing for transferring an image.

GRAVELS Commercial gravels, or 'pea' gravel, naturally worn by the sea, are used as aggregates or for texture in mosaic.

GRAZING See *nibbling.*

GREEK KEY PATTERN Popular name for maeander, a much-used mosaic border decoration

Granite
Faille III, 1998 by Henry-Noel Aubry, 120cm x 100cm / 47in x 39in, marble, granite and slate.

The French artist Henry-Noel Aubry was born in 1960 in Provence and studied at l'Ecole des Beaux Arts in Paris. It was there in the studio of Riccardo Licata that he had his first encounter with mosaic, a physical one that was a turning point in his life. The series Faille, meaning fault, flow or weakness, has engaged Aubry for many years. Begun as an homage to the earth, he has developed a geological/visual dialogue. He delights in exploring natural materials – granite, travertine, volcanic lava, onyx, and in particular slate – revelling in their colours and characteristic qualities. Each mosaic allows time to reflect; the formation of rocks acquired naturally through time takes on new significance in this artist's hands.

in Greek and Roman times, often used as a running frieze. It is also known as Greek fret or Roman key design, and continues to be a popular pattern.

GREEK MYTH Narratives, commonly understood by Ancient Greeks, connected with their ideas about the past and religion. The epic tales that evolved of gods and heroes were developed among educated sections of the population in Roman times, and often manifested themselves in pebble and stone mosaics, particularly tales from the two great epic poems, *The Iliad* and *The Odyssey*, works probably of the late 8th century BC attributed to Homer.

GRID A symmetrical scheme of squares or rectangles.

GRINDER An electrical smoothing tool. **See *emery paper*.**

GRINDING WHEEL A machine, only occasionally used, for the smooth finishing of mosaic edges after cutting. **See *carborundum; finish*.**

GROUT / GROUTING (It. *stuccatura / masticatura*) Generally understood to be a mixture of sand, cement (often 3–4 parts sand : 1 part cement), and water, with or without colour, which is worked or pressed into the gaps or interstices between the mosaic tesserae to give mosaic its traditional characteristic 'look' after the mosaic has been made – it gives strength, smoothness and general cohesion and permanence to a mosaic, especially in hard-wearing conditions (floors, pools, pathways, etc.). There are various grouts for normal interstices to which colour can be added. Use a fine-textured grout for gaps up to 4mm / $^3/_{16}$in and a coarser textured grout for up to 12mm / $^1/_2$in gaps, and add flexible admixes if necessary (see flexible bonding). Always read packaging information carefully. Ready-mixed grouts are also available. Wall grouts are generally white (which can be coloured) and there are also fine-textured grouts for easy cleaning of surfaces. Epoxy grouts are those used for interior and exterior locations, specially formulated to provide a durable, hygienic and abrasion-resistant surface. Epoxy grouts are able to resist moisture, chemicals, solvents and oil, and are therefore used where food is prepared (kitchens), or where there is water (baths, showers). Some practitioners of today, as in Byzantium, prefer not to grout, especially where it is felt colour or intensity of the surface of the material is reduced or devalued. **See *epoxy resin*.**

GROUT FLOAT See *float*.

GROUT PIGMENT Grout has been coloured since ancient times – a house threshold at Olynthos in northern Greece, 5th century BC, has a whitish blue marble floor with a distinctive red grout as an integral part of the design. Also in the Rotondo of the early Christian Church of Santo Stefano in Rome a yellow ochre has been used to colour the mortar mix; the setting bed acts here as a grout since the mortar is pushed upwards between the tesserae on setting. **See *pigments*.**

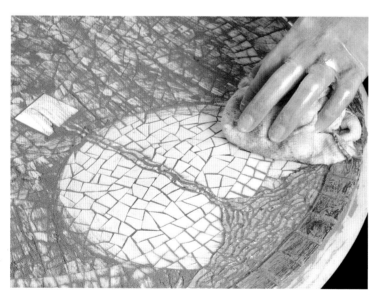

Grout
A proprietary grout with no added colour was mixed with a little water. Too much water at this stage would weaken the porosity of the grout and be liable to shrink when setting. The mix was stiffer than normal, since the base of the mosaic is marble and non-porous and therefore allowed for no water absorption from the mix, as would happen on a wooden support. The grout was pressed into all the interstices, taking care over any raised areas. When cleaned using a squeegee and rags, equal care was taken around both protruding and sunken areas, ensuring that each tessera was wiped clean of the grout. (JM)

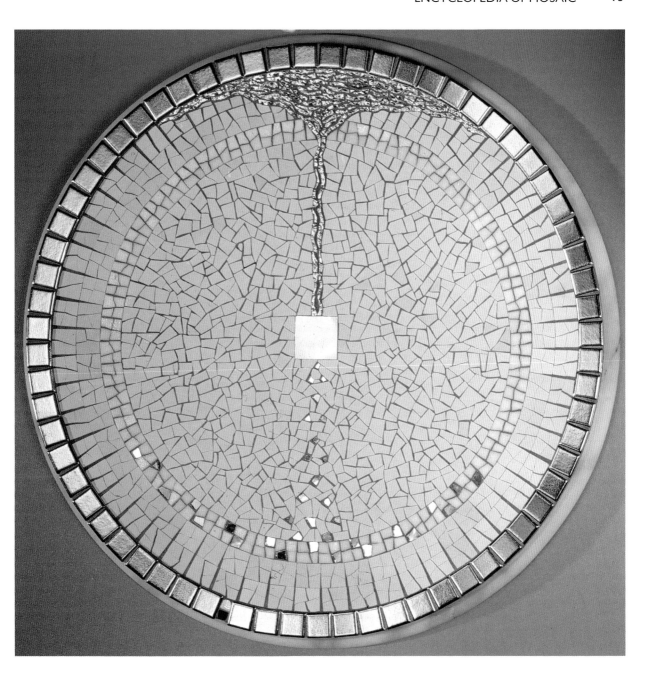

Grout

Mensa Muse (table top), 2001 by Elaine M Goodwin, 60cm / 24in diameter, matt and glazed ceramic tiles, Venetian gold, vitreous glass, mirror. (Private collection.) (JM)

The mosaic, after grouting, was attached to a base of iron to create a circular table, by the artist Elaine M Goodwin for an exhibition in Luxembourg, entitled Salutations to the Muse, in 2001. The artist makes occasional functional or utilitarian mosaics, delighting to see mosaic, especially her beloved gold, sat upon, eaten off or walked over in a domestic or everyday setting. To grout or not to grout? – a question often asked by artists when considering their mosaic. For practical surfaces, i.e. floors, paving, tables, food surfaces, etc., where the mosaic is functional, grouting the mosaic is essential in giving a watertight, smooth and strong surface, and also imparting a traditional, characteristic mosaic look.

GROUT SPONGE See *builder's sponge.*

GROUT SQUEEGEE A tool often having a wooden handle of 20cm / 8in and a rubber blade, for spreading grout over a mosaic or tile surface.

GUIDELINES Linear indications for mosaicists in Roman times that would be scored into the wet mortar (examples can be seen at Rudston, Yorkshire, UK); or painted (as in the red paint in Cirencester, Gloucester, UK); or executed in charcoal (as can be made out on the brickwork of the dome of the Rotunda in Thessalonika, Greece, where the mosaic has become detached and drawings of the angel wings are easily discerned). Artists today employ guidelines particularly when executing large-scale works, using paint and/or indelible pens.

GUILLOCHE A form of interlaced or twisted bands or braiding; a plait pattern made of two or more interweaving strands of interlacing or twisted forms, and a very popular border design in ancient, especially Roman, mosaics. **See *cable pattern.***

GUM ARABIC A natural glue that is extracted from the sap of the acacia tree and used with water for a watersoluble adhesive. Nowadays readily prepared synthetic and cellulose gums are available for the same use. Angelo Orsoni Mosaic in Venice gave me this recipe for preparing the glue to be used to stick mosaics on to paper for the indirect method. Ingredients: 1kg / 2.2lb flour, a spoonful of honey, half a spoonful of glycerine, half a spoonful of powdered gum arabic (or ratios thereof). Put all the ingredients into a large saucepan together with one and a half litres (2 and a half pints) of water, heat and stir until the mixture is even. Simmer while stirring continuously for up to 45 minutes without ever allowing it to boil. Take from the heat and continue to stir the mix until completely cold in order to avoid hardening of the surface; in the end the mixture should have the consistency of a sauce such as mayonnaise. The glue can then be laid on to the sheet of paper with a brush, which should not be too soft. You may find you need a little more water and less stirring time!

GUNITE CEMENT A liquid cement, generally used for large external 2D or 3D mosaics. It is sprayed on to a prepared surface and leaves a smooth finish on which to put a mosaic.

Gunite cement
La Force – in preparation 1987 by Niki de Saint Phalle, Detail, from 'Il Giardino dei Tarocchi', Tuscany, Italy. (EMG)

Many of the large works constructed in this garden have an iron armature, acting as reinforcement for the cement cladding that gives the works their form. When construction was complete a fine mortar was mixed and was carried in large tanks to the sculptures, which were sprayed to give a smooth, thin finishing veneer.

Gunite cement
La Force, Card no. 11, 1990s by Niki de Saint Phalle, from the Tarot Garden, Tuscany, Italy (EMG).

French artist Niki de Saint Phalle (1930–2002) was an artist extraordinaire. She was born in Paris and brought up in New York. With an instinctive drive she worked in the media of assemblage, sculpture, relief and mosaic. In 1980 she began work on a sculpture garden in Tuscany, taking inspiration from the Tarot pack of cards. Twenty-two sculptures were constructed, conceived as free-standing and architectural works, some in collaboration with the French sculptor Jean Tinguely. Much of the work has a mosaic finish in tiles (many handmade). Coloured mirror and glass in all forms create an external space of mystery and ambiguity.

HAMMER, MOSAIC (It. *martellina* f.) A curved hammer with two sharpened cutting edges tipped with tungsten-carbide alloy. It can be made of any weight according to the artist's preference, approx. 1kg / 2.2lb. Other hammers that are used in making mosaics are scaling hammers, chipping hammers and lump hammers. In the Museo de Ostia near Rome, Italy, there is a *bas-relief* of mosaic cutters from the late 2nd or early 3rd century. It is a unique representation showing the making of mosaics. The work depicts two seated cutters using hammers, one from the left-hand side and one from the right-hand side, one with a basket of tesserae beside him. In the background two men can be seen carrying away sacks (of tesserae?). An indigo blue was rubbed into the background. Cutting is the same procedure as today – a timeless and perpetually modern art form!

HANGING MOSAICS Many modern mosaics are hung as pictures on a wall. In each case, the choice of positioning drastically changes the way a work is seen or read. Any work that uses reflective material such as mirror, glass, gold or other metals should have special attention paid to its siting. Experiment with placing a work opposite a light source, adjacent to it or at an angle to it, and vary the position and height for maximum subtlety or impact.

HARDIE (It. *tagliolo* m.) A tool that looks like an inverted chisel, with the curved cutting edge made of tungsten-carbide for strength and sharpness. It is fixed into wood, most often a wooden tree trunk or a heavy portable block, which is then set at a comfortable height for use either sitting or standing. There are two different kinds of hardie for cutting: (a) glass, e.g. smalti; and (b) stone, marble, pebbles, etc. The material to be cut is placed on top of the chisel blade and held between finger and thumb. The hammer, held in the opposite hand, falls directly on to the centre of the material from above, with a light but firm blow. It is advisable always to cut in half each time until the required size of the material/tessera is achieved. Practice will be needed, but great accuracy and speed are soon reached. Also known as a pin.

Hammer and hardie – demonstration
(*Left*) **(JM)** The hammer blow is swift and sure, to be certain of cutting the marble cube directly in half with a clean cut. Dust flies everywhere, so wear a dust mask if cutting a large number of tesserae.

Hammer and hardie
(*Right*) **(JM)**
The artist, Elaine M Goodwin, in her UK studio, cutting rosa portogallo marble tesserae with a marble-cutting hardie, which has a much broader chisel cutting edge than a smaller, slimmer, smalto-cutting hardie. The wooden trunk support is gripped with the knees and the hammer raised directly above the tessera, which is placed in the centre of the chisel edge and held by finger and thumb. The mosaic in the background, made in part with this beautiful pink-coloured crystalline marble, is entitled And You!, and was made by the artist in 2002.

HELLENIC (adj.) Greek, used in particular of civilization from the fall of the Mycenaeans in the 12th century BC until the demise of Alexander the Great, 323 BC. From *Hellas*, Greece.

HELLENISTIC The civilization of Greece and the Eastern Mediterranean world between the death of Alexander the Great and the Roman conquest of the region, that is from 323 BC to the 1st century BC. Geographically it generally refers to the area under the rule of Alexander's successors. From *Hellenize*, to adopt a Greek style.

HESSIAN A loose-woven material attached with adhesive to the surface of a mosaic to help in transferring a work, or lifting to place in a permanent position. **See *gauze fabric.***

HIPPOCAMPUS (or sea horse) An animal motif that appears on marine scenes in ancient mosaics. Its front half is a horse while its rear half is a spiralling tail.

HISTORICAL SOURCES (of mosaic) There have been, and are, many scholars of and writers on mosaic, from the early mention of pavements by Pliny the Elder (AD 23–79) in his *Historia Naturalis* [Natural History], and some passages in *Vitrivius De Architectura* [On Architecture], late 1st century BC. Diocletian's *Edictum de Pretiis* [Edict on Prices], AD 301, is a fascinating read on the maximum payment of mosaicists; e.g. the *pictor imaginarius*, who was the creator of the cartoon and devised the colours, was paid around 175 *sesterces* per day; the *pictor pavietarius* who transferred the cartoon to wall or pavement, 75 *s.p.d.*; the *calcis costor*, who prepared the cement, 60 *s.p.d.*; the *pavimentarius*, who prepared the bed surface, 50–60 *s.p.d.*; the *tessellarius*, who made the simpler parts of the mosaic, 50–60 *s.p.d.*; and the *musearius*, who made the more complex parts and figures of the mosaic, 50–60 *s.p.d.* During the Renaissance, the effusive writer and artist Giorgio Vasari included mosaic in his book on painting, architecture and sculpture, entitled *De Technica* [On Technique]. More recently, from the 20th century up to the present, scholars and authors on history and techniques of mosaic have made great efforts to co-ordinate knowledge and terminology (often very confused) and at the same time to keep alive the interest and intrigue that surrounds mosaic work of each era. For modern mosaic one author – the late Peter Fischer – stands apart, with his work of 1971 on *The History and Technique of Mosaic* (translated and revised from the German of his earlier book *Das Mosaik*, 1969, pub. Anton Scholla, Vienna and Munich), which has been used as a standard reference to the present day.

HOLOGRAPHIC MOSAIC A form of mosaic that uses holograms and holographic imagery, often combined with other materials, to produce a surface which, like smalti and mirror, dematerializes a surface but also deceives the eye with an apparent 3D appearance. The tesserae are made by cutting holograms from credit cards, gift wrap and cosmetic cartons, etc., and fixing them on lightweight backing materials (see pages 80–81).

HOMER Greek poet, believed to have composed the epic poems *The Iliad* and *The Odyssey,* which date from around the late 8th century BC, and that gave rise to a great deal of mythological imagery used in mosaic flooring.

HORTUS CONCLUSUS An enclosed garden.

HUE The basic attribute of colour, e.g. yellow, red, blue. **See *colour.***

Historical sources (of mosaic)
Peter Fischer in 1997, St Mark's Square Venice, Italy, photographed by the author. Born in 1922 in Brieg (which was then in Germany and is now in Poland), Peter Fischer lived from 1956 in London, England. He is the author of the 1971 standard text *The History and Technique of Mosaic.* He died in 2000. (EMG)

HYDRATED LIME Lime, with added water, that has been allowed to dry and is then crumbled into a powder form for mosaic use. See *'aged' lime.*

HYDRAULIC BINDER A binder that hardens under water as well as in the air. Portland cement is one such substance as is aluminous cement.

HYDROCHLORIC ACID (muriatic acid, spirits of salt) HCl; dilute 1 : 20 (acid to water). This is an effective substance, used for cleaning cement residue on mosaic surfaces and traces of lime mortar film. Gently brush the surface of the mosaic with the acid (wearing protective gloves). Leave a few seconds, then wash off with copious amounts of water to neutralize the acid; if at all uncertain of a thorough cleaning, make up a mix of baking soda and water (250 ml = 1 large teaspoonful), and brush on to the surface and wash off. Other cleaners or products that can be used and are easily available include masonry, brick or patio cleaners and concrete cleansers, where HCl is mixed with water and cleaning agents. Use on concrete, terracotta, glass and stone surfaces, but not on marble or other calcareous stones. In all cases rinse thoroughly and repeatedly with water.

Holographic mosaic
Making Waves, detail, 1997 by Jan Williams, Café Bar, Quay Arts, Isle of Wight, UK, 212cm^2 / 32$^{3/4}$in^2, holograms, mixed media.

The English artist Jan Williams (b. 1967) lives and works in Portsmouth, when not travelling around the country with her Caravan Gallery, recording the 'real' Britain. Her mosaics are constructed from an assemblage of materials from which her tesserae are cut, frequently incorporating 20th- and 21st-century debris such as drink cans, crisp packets and discarded credit cards. The resulting surfaces seduce the eye from afar and intrigue with close scrutiny.

ICON (mosaic icon) A luxury portable object for private Christian devotion, from the late Byzantine era. They were regarded as a testimony to the presence of the Divine – and also as intermediaries between the human and the celestial. A fine 14th-century mosaic example of a Madonna and Child is in the Byzantine Museum in Athens, Greece.

ICONOCLASM A religious movement of the 8th and 9th centuries which denied the holiness of icons and forbade image veneration. There were two periods, 730–87, and 814–43. Many mosaics with figurative elements were defaced, and replaced with crudely filled areas of tesserae or other images. Examples can be seen in the 8th-century AD Church on the Acropolis at Ma'in, west of Madaba, Jordan.

IMPLUVIUM A shallow pool in an atrium of a Roman villa used to catch rainwater.

IMPREGNATOR A liquid solution that is applied to slate, stones, and other porous surfaces to make them resistant to external marking and staining and the weather. Use a brush or soft cloth to apply the solution to a dry, clean surface, making two or three applications if necessary, for an increased non-absorbent (impermeable) surface – don't overdo! **See *sealers.***

IMPRESSED TILE (counter-relief) A tile with a line decoration formed by using metal moulds, which raises the outline of the design on the surface.

INDIRECT / INVERTED TECHNIQUE (It. *metodo indiretto / rovescio* – reverse transfer method) A technique in which the tesserae are fixed only temporarily on to paper. A strong backing paper is laid on a smooth surface. The design is then drawn in reverse, i.e. right to left, with clear indication lines as to form, direction, flow or colour. If a large piece is to be done, various sections will be designed and cut; they can be up to 65cm / 25^1/$_2$in for ease of portability and transportation. On the back of each paper section scribbled registration marks should be drawn to act as aids when fitting the various sections together. Keep a key drawing of the whole work and its numbered sections for reference and when putting together.

The tesserae are attached to the paper, with their smooth side face down, using a watersoluble adhesive, such as gum arabic or wheat flour glue (not too much), that is fairly slow-drying to allow for repositioning and correcting while work is in progress. Leave gaps between the tesserae, and allow to dry completely. There are various methods of fixing: (1) trowel a layer of adhesive or cement on to the surface to receive the mosaic; and / or (2) trowel a thin area of adhesive or cement on to the tesserae on the paper.

Carefully lift, invert and place the papered mosaic into position and tap in place with a flat piece of wood, gently tamping with a hammer to give an even surface. Allow to dry, but, if using cement mortar, not to set. Using a builder's sponge, moisten the paper, and after a short while peel it off; this is the time to make final adjustments if any movement or displacement of tesserae has occurred. The advantages of this technique are that work can be of any size, and fitted to a great variety of surfaces, including convex and concave sites, e.g. columns, vaults, niches. The disadvantages are that work done in this way often lacks a liveliness of surface, as the tesserae are set completely flat on to the paper and the play of light over the surface is restricted. **See *methods; laying.***

Indirect method
Various Moments in the Day of a Lady of Fashion, detail, 1922 by Boris Anrep, Birmingham Museums and Art Gallery, England. (EMG)

The Russian artist Boris Anrep (1885–1969) studied in St Petersburg (Russia), Paris (France), and Edinburgh College of Art (Scotland), before living and working in England and then France. He worked on many major commissions in England, including the floor of the National Gallery in London, 1928–33, and the walls of Westminster Cathedral, 1924, 1956–62. He believed mosaic should introduce colour into buildings and that the materials of the tesserae should be integral with those of the surrounding architecture. He was one of the first modern mosaic artists to both design and execute a work himself, often in collaboration with Justin Vulliamy and other assistants. He preferred the indirect or transfer method of working, away from site – but was ever conscious of the importance of the surface texture, although the effects of colour were his main consideration.

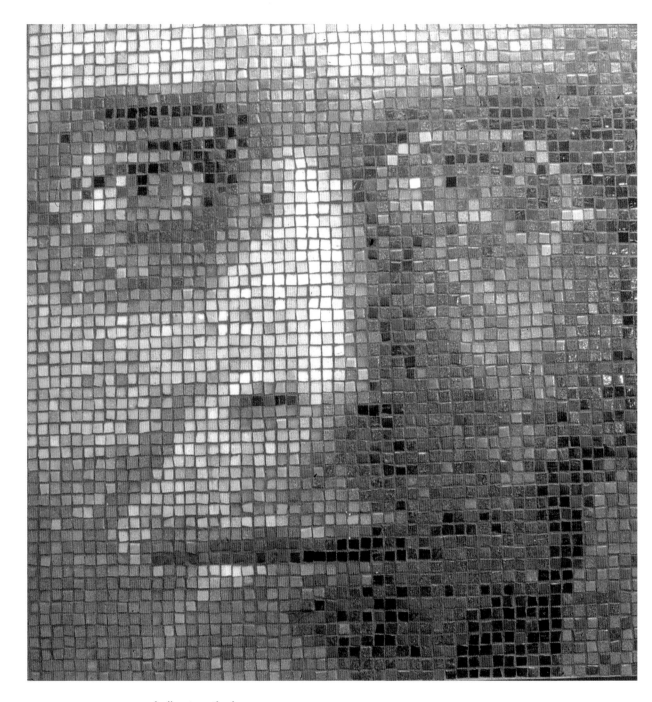

Indirect method
The Bishop, 2000 by Tessa Hunkin, 75cm x 75cm / 30in x 30in, vitreous glass.

The English artist Tessa Hunkin lives and works in London. In the 1980s she, with her friend and work partner Emma Biggs, set up Mosaic Workshop to work on large-scale mosaics. The company has flourished, and alongside creating mosaics to commission, runs courses and generally inspires would-be mosaicists to know about their art form. Great advocates of Boris Anrep, they specialize in the indirect method of mosaic making, thereby continuing the tradition for large-scale murals constructed in a studio and erected on site.

INLAY An object set into the surface of a larger object.

INSULA (Latin) A tenement block or block of houses in Roman times.

INTAGLIO A sunk or negative relief, the opposite to 'cameo', which is a raised or positive relief.

INTARSIA (also *tarsia / intarsiatura*) A form of inlay, whereby shaped designs of stone, ivory, metal and wood, etc., are inlaid into a prepared background. It is a form of mosaic inlay, planed and polished smooth, not forming the whole surface. **See *commesso work.***

INTENSITY (of a colour) The saturation or brightness of a colour.

INTERIOR MOSAIC (interior design) The term generally applied today to works made for a specific location or on a particular theme or colour scheme for an interior setting. This may be for a commercial or domestic situation. Many mosaicists work for a domestic market, designing and executing mosaics for homes, offices and restaurants. Often functional, such works may include tables, chairs, mirrors and bar furniture.

INTERSTICES In mosaic, the spaces or gaps between the surface tesserae. They can be of various widths and colour-grouted. They are of major importance in considering the initial design of the mosaic.

INTERVALS In a mosaic, the space between the main elements of a design that give it rhythm.

IRIDESCENCE A colour band or rainbow effect sometimes seen on the surface of glass. It is due to the refraction of light. Some mosaicists are attracted to iridescent stained glass and utilize this effect in their work.

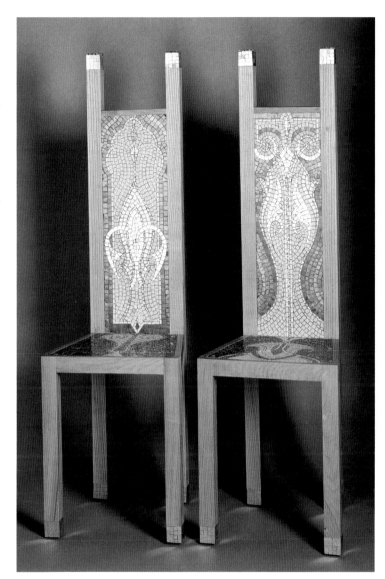

Interior mosaic
He and *She*, 2001 by Elaine M Goodwin, 36cm x 123cm x 36cm / 14in x 4ft 1in x 14in, chairs designed by EMG, made by Vic Mousel in ash wood. Mosaic materials: Venetian metallic gold leaf, ceramic. (Private collection.) (JM)

The author makes occasional forays into mosaic making for interiors. The pair of chairs continues a much-explored theme of the artist, the male/female. She enjoys watching which sex sits on which chair! The inspiration for the design was gathered in Morocco, a country in which the artist also lives and works.

JEWEL A piece of pre-shaped faceted glass created in a variety of colours and shapes, e.g. circle, square. See *globs*.

JUSTINIAN The renowned Byzantine emperor, AD 527–565, who initiated the first golden age of Byzantine art, which continued, with two breaks of iconoclasm between 730 and 843 when there were bans on religious images. (The second golden age was from the late 9th to the 13th century, when Byzantium was under Western rule until 1261. The third golden age occurred under the Palaeologan dynasty, which fell in 1453 to the Ottoman sultan, Mehmet II.)

JUXTAPOSITION The use of differing colours in close proximity. In mosaic this was first used in early Byzantine times for enhancement and optical effect. The only mixing of colours in mosaic is done with the eye, as separate units of colour of similar or complementary hue are laid alongside each other for mutual or singular colour intensification. This understanding of colour application was only to be really regained in the late 19th century, when colour theory was developed by scientists and artists. See *divisionism; optical mixing; pointillism; secondary colours.*

Justinian
The Emperor Justinian, detail, S. Vitale, Ravenna, Italy, mid-6th century, smalti, marble, mother of pearl. (EMG)

Justinian, a Latin speaker, was obsessed with the ideal of the Roman Empire. His reign was based in Constantinople, from where he began an ambitious campaign to build for posterity, traces of which can be seen today throughout the Mediterranean, e.g. Istanbul (Constantinople), Jerusalem, Ephesus and Ravenna. The mosaic is a detail of one of two facing panels in the church of San Vitale. It is a masterly portrait containing just enough allusion to the real, yet achieving an almost iconic quality. The richness of the coloured smalti is enhanced by a golden background of slightly angled tesserae – a ground much favoured by the Byzantine mosaicist for its dispersal of light, evoking spiritual contemplation.

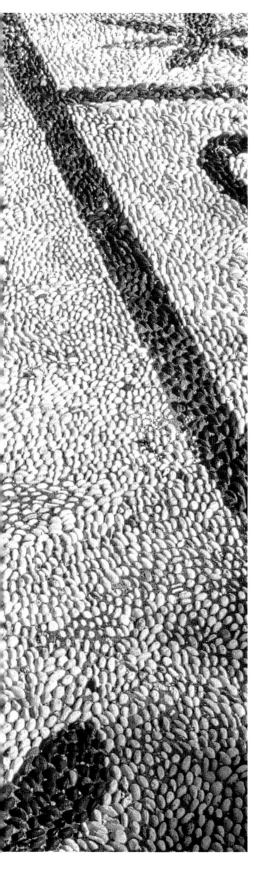

KANTHAROS (Gk.) / **CANTHARUS** (L.) A wine cup with high volute handles, used as a decorative motif in many ancient mosaics.

KILN A specialist apparatus used for creating personalized tesserae. The choice of kiln – top loader or front loader, electric, oil-fired or gas-fired – will depend on usage and price. Kilns can be used for clay firing, glazing, glass fusions and enamelling.

KNAPPING HAMMER A hammer used to break stones and natural materials, by snapping them in two, particularly flint and slate.

KNIFE These are many and often indispensable, e.g. putty knife, craft knife etc. The great variety of blades and edges are used for cutting, scoring and drawing on cement or wood. A great number will be amassed!

KRATER / CRATER A wide-mouthed vase or bowl for mixing wine and water, used as an image in Greek and Roman mosaics, often with a vine spiralling from its mouth, e.g. the Dionysus mosaics of Sousse and El Djem, Tunisia, 2nd and 3rd century.

KROKALIA (croclakia, hohlakia) Decorative pebble mosaics traditionally used in gardens, courtyards and houses in Greece from the 17th century, particularly in the islands of the Dodecanese. The pebble mosaics used geometry or symbolic imagery in colours of black and white with some addition of red.

Krokalia
At the Church of the Metamorfosis in Hermoupolis, on the island of Syros in Greece, the courtyard is embellished by decorative pavements with designs of flowers, trees, snake forms and geometric designs. The pebbles were collected from the Greek islands and laid, uncut, directly into a cement mortar. They are of small size, approx. 4cm/1 ¹/₂in in length and mostly of black colour, with a few strategically placed red pebbles on a white ground. (EMG)

LACED / LACE-MOSAIC BOWL A bowl with glass strips laid side by side across it instead of in a spiral. These twists of opaque glass were popular in the 1st century AD in decorative glass vessels.

LACONICUM   A room in a Roman bathhouse (*thermae*) for taking steam baths.

LACUNA A term used by mosaic conservators for a missing area of a damaged mosaic. These are generally left as such, i.e. not filled in with a supposed design. It is general practice to infill the space with a mortar of a complementary colour to the remaining mosaic and finish to a smooth surface.

LAMINATED BOARD   Also blockboard / particle board. These are boards made up of strips of wood or flax particles bonded together with synthetic resins, which can be used for interior mosaic making.

LAMINATION   The use of a thin rectangular strip of stone or other material to create a smooth surface.

LAPILLI   Small pebbles; used in making an early type of mosaic flooring. Listels (strips) of lead or clay guide the pebbles so that they follow an underlying drawing; e.g. at Pella, 4th century BC, northern Greece. **See** *pebble mosaic.*

LATERICIUM See *opus latericium.*

LATEX   A naturally occurring ingredient used in adhesive mortars for use on plywood and wood finishes where greater flexibility is needed. It is often white and can be coloured with pigments as necessary.

LATEX CEMENT   By adding liquid latex to a dry mortar mix of sand and cement in lieu of water, a strong, flexible setting cement bed for mosaic is made. Many brands have proprietary mixes.

LAVA PESTA   A pavement mortar with added aggregate using a large quantity of volcanic lava.

LAYING   Also setting, (em)bedding, placing, applying. There are many methods of laying mosaic work. If using (1) a mosaic pre-prepared directly on net, this may be laid on to a concrete setting bed. The area should be brushed clean and soaked with water. A 'screed' made of sand and cement is then prepared, leaving up to a 1.5cm / ⅝in allowance for the finished mosaic. If the area is very large, divide it into sections using plastic, metal or greased wood strips. When the screed has cured, soak with water and brush over with a slurry of sand, cement and extra water, and place the netted mosaic on to the slurry. When it has 'held', grout and clean. If using (2) the double reverse method, sketch a design in a tray of fine sand, and then place the tesserae on it, face up. When completed, glue strong paper or muslin (cheesecloth) to the surface. Be sure to stick to every tessera using a brush loaded with gum arabic or other temporary adhesive such as paste, or flour and water. When set, the panel is lifted out of the sand and reset: if on to concrete, as above for a permanent position; if, however, laying into an epoxy or synthetic resin base, be sure to brush away any moist sand and dry thoroughly before fixing. If using (3) the indirect method, take a piece of linen, cloth, paper, etc., and draw on the design. Then, with a temporary glue, fix the tesserae face down. When set, the whole is lifted and reversed at site and set into its permanent position, the right way up. Once set, moisten the temporary backing material and peel off, then grout as above. Be sure to remove all traces of any outline of individual panels if a composite design is made. Try to make sectional panels in all cases empathetic with the design – i.e. cut sections along main drawing lines, if possible; if not, leave out some of the tesserae near the joins and fix after setting into the final position. In this way the sectional panel will not be seen to be made up of units but as one uniform panel. **See** *direct method; indirect; double reverse; setting mosaics.*

LEAD STRIPS   Narrow strips of lead are seen on mosaics in Pella, Greece (4th century BC), and in Hellenistic mosaics in North Africa, especially Alexandria. They are placed for outlining and emphasis, and to enhance the aesthetic possibilities. If using them today, shape them and place them in position before working up to their edges. **See** *calm.*

LETTERING The specific use of letters in a mosaic – this may be for a sign, a logo, a nameplate or a multitude of other reasons.

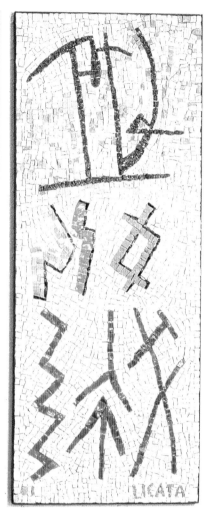

Lettering
Trittico, 2001 by Riccardo Licata, 100cm x 120cm / 39in x 48in, marble and smalti.

The Italian artist was born in Turin (1929) and trained in part at the Accademia di Belle Arti in Venice, Italy. In 1957 he joined the great Italian artist and mosaic *supremo* Gino Severini (1883–1966) at his Italian Mosaic School in Paris, France. In 1958 he succeeded Severini and initiated the Mosaic workshop at the Ecole Nationale Supérieure des Beaux Arts in Paris, where he taught and inspired many of today's leading mosaic artists until his retirement in 1995. His works are characterized by a personalized hieroglyphic – an abstract writing in mosaic, lyrical and mysteriously didactic – enjoyed through the rhythm of colour and materials that shape his language.

LIFTING The removal of a mosaic from its site; it is then replaced, usually in another position, e.g. the Low Ham 'Dido and Aeneas' mosaic, now in Taunton museum, UK. Many Greek and Roman mosaics were lifted this way and repositioned at municipal museums. The floor is cleaned, and fabric is attached to the surface with an adhesive that is temporary. This is then backed with a stronger cloth. Panels of large size are cut and divided with copper strips. One panel is moved at a time and, with the help of chisels or long steel blades, the tesserae are loosened from their base and the mortar into which they were attached, and removed panel by panel before re-siting. In the mid-20th century, mosaics were removed as a whole, and rolled up like a carpet on huge rollers.

LIGHTING See *hanging mosaics*.

LIME A material obtained by firing limestone at a high temperature. Quicklime is the term applied to the first substance after firing. When water is added it swells and becomes hydrated, giving out heat, and when dried becomes a powder. When water is added to this it is called 'slaked' lime. When sand is added it becomes a very hard substance as a result of carbonization, and when used as a filler, becomes very long-lasting. Lime can also be used for a setting plaster for mosaics. Therefore it is thought of as a binder that is malleable and hardens in air but is dissolved by water. If it is used with sand and cement it gives excellent workable results ($^3/_4$ sand, 1 cement, 1 lime). See *'aged lime'; lime putty*.

LIME PLASTER Lime does not occur naturally but is obtained by calcination of calcium carbonate. When roasted it gives off CO_2 – and calcium oxide. $CaCO_3 +$ heat $\rightarrow CaO + CO_2$. If water is added, it creates a crumbling powder and slaked lime + heat: $CaO + H_2O \rightarrow Ca(OH)_2 +$ heat. But add more water and some grit and a building mortar is obtained: $Ca(OH)_2 + CO_2 \rightarrow CaCO_3 + H_2O$. This lime plaster is commonly used in mosaic making. See *cement mortar*.

LIME PUTTY Hydrated lime, with enough water to make it pliable and easy to work. It is sometimes mixed with sand as a temporary binder for setting mosaics. See *'aged' lime*.

LINEAR MOSAIC One which is dominated by line (rather than colour or form).

LISIBILITY This term refers to how a mosaic floor can be 'read' from many vantage points as, for example, in ornamental or geometrical mosaics; or from one viewpoint only, as in threshold mosaics or many triclinium mosaics where the often figurative emblema can be seen 'the right way up' from one point only, and from the side or even upside down from another. The couches were often arranged for best viewing when reclining. See *trompe l'oeil*.

LITHOSTROTON (Gk. *lithos*, a stone and *strotos*, spread; from *stronnumi*, to spread) 'Strewn-stone'; a paving with small irregular pieces of stone, patternless, and often of different colours. In ancient times the term was used to describe mosaic and tessellated pavements or floors made of marble or limestone slabs or plates.

LUMINOSITY In mosaic this can be created by placing certain colours adjacent to each other, for spatial and light or airy effects.

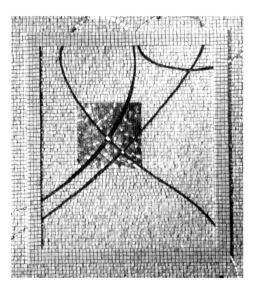

Linear Mosaic
String Theory I, 2001 by Elaine M. Goodwin. Private collection. 80cm x 88cm / 32 x 34in, carrarra marble, Venetian gold, fool's gold.

One of a series of three panels taking communication as a theme and allowing the line to dominate in the work.

LUNETTE The semicircular area of wall at the end of a vaulted ceiling – a popular architectural position for mosaics, both religious and secular.

LUSTRE A decorative effect of rich iridescent sheen. In glassmaking it is a finish made by mixing metallic salts with the surface glaze. Colours can include gold, blue, green, red, etc.

LUSTRE-WARE A ceramic ware or mosaic tile with a metallic or iridescent finish that can be cut and used to create areas of interest in a work.

Luminosity (above)
Iridescent Circle, 2001 by Giulio Candussio, diameter 200cm / 80in, smalti, marble.

The Italian artist Giulio Candussio was born in Udine (1945) and attended the acclaimed Mosaic School in Spilimbergo as pupil and teacher. An experimenter, he has continually explored the mosaic medium to find a personal language. In 1980 he became an art director for the huge mosaic company Bisazza, where he continued in experimental vein, realizing the Eduardo Paolozzi mosaic from design to mosaic for Tottenham Court Road underground station in London (1983). His evolving mosaic enquiry into techniques and application, enhanced by his teaching skills, has made him an artist of surety and surprise.

MAENAD A female devotee of the god Dionysus or Bacchus, often portrayed dancing in Greek and Roman mosaics, e.g. Olynthos, Greece.

MAGNESITE Magnesium oxychloride is a binding material that was used in the mid-20th century to fix mosaic materials to wood and metal. One part of magnesium oxychloride crystals is mixed with water. When the crystals have dissolved, the mix is gently heated and one part of magnesite with a lime-proof colour pigment (if needed) is added and mixed to a malleable consistency. It is not easy to use, but provides an excellent binder in interior, dry conditions. The recipe was a favourite of American artist Jeanne Reynal, but the binder has been superseded by the versatile and flexible proprietary cement adhesives of today.

MAJOLICA TECHNIQUE To make personalized tiles for mosaic use, place or overlap a small quantity of stained glass or smalti on white commercial tiles, and melt in a kiln at temperatures of about 1050ºC / 1922ºF) to obtain a mix of vibrant and exciting textures. Cut and use as required.

MAJOLICA TILES Tiles with an opaque brightly coloured surface glaze, often in relief.

MAQUETTE A project, usually a small model, that serves as a point of departure for a finished work. See *bozzetto*.

MARBLE A limestone, made of calcite or dolomite crystals. It has always been used extensively in mosaic making, cut into tesserae for pavements and employed traditionally in the faces, hands and white robes of figures in the Byzantine era. It is enjoying a rebirth in modern mosaic making. Some favoured marbles include:

white marbles: (i) Parian marble, from the island of Paros, a brilliant translucent white and of large crystalline structure; (ii) Pentelic marble found near Athens, a fine-grained marble that develops a yellow patina; (iii) Carrara (Luna) marble, fine-grained from the Apuan Alps near Carrara, and (iv) Thasos, a brilliant white with large crystals from the Greek island of that name.

black marbles: bigio antico from Cape Taenarum in the Peloponnese.

red marbles: (i) rosso antico from Southern Greece, and (ii) porphyry from Egypt (quite purplish).

white/blue/violet marbles: pavonazzetto, from Dokimeion in Turkey (Phrygian marble).

light green marbles: cipollino, from south-east Euboea.

creamy white marbles: giallo antico from Chemtou, Tunisia (this can also be gold and orange).

green marbles: verde antico and broccatello.

Marble may be used in an unpolished state, tumbled (i.e. distressed with water and sand), or used with rounded edges. It is generally cut with a hammer and hardie, or with a watercooled diamond cutting wheel.

Maquette
Obelisk, 2001 by Elaine M Goodwin, 43cm x 178cm / 17in x 70in, ceramic, Venetian gold/silver. (JM)

In 2000 the author, artist Elaine M Goodwin was commissioned to create a work for the Mediterranean Biome for the Eden Project in St Austell, England. Given 'the olive' as her plant to interpret, the artist chose to make a mosaic triptych entitled *Liquid Gold*. Beginning with a square of Venetian gold to represent the olive, the work unfolded as a 36m / 120ft pavement with a central river of gold, with broad ceramic edgings in white, interspersed with 22 evenly spaced white mosaic doves, obliquely seen and representing each Mediterranean country. The olive tree itself manifests as an obelisk, for which this maquette was made and enabled experiment with size, materials and technique.

Maquette
Liquid Gold, triptych, 2001 by Elaine M Goodwin, Eden Project, St Austell, Cornwall, England, Venetian gold, ceramic. (JM)

The mosaic *Liquid Gold* in situ at the Eden Project in Cornwall, a living theatre of plants and people. The two Biomes, one for tropical plants and the one above for Mediterranean plants, were designed by the architect Nicholas Grimshaw, inspired by the vision of Tim Smit. Daylight, or light from the sun, an ever-changing phenomenon in an English climate, strikes the metallic surfaces of the triptych to create areas of brilliant light or glowing sheen. It is rare to catch the effects of natural light in an exposed if protected position, on such an expanse of gold – one usually reserved for religious interiors in arches and domes.

Marble
Paysage de l'âme, 2000 by Giovanna Galli, 60cm x 60cm / 24in x 24in, marble, granite, stone.

The Italian artist Giovanna Galli was born in Ravenna, Italy (1953) where she studied mosaic before attending the Ecole des Beaux Arts in the studio of Riccardo Licata in Paris, France, where she continues to live and work. Skilled in restoration, and a versatile artist and author, she often collaborates with other artists in the realization of mosaic projects. Her personal work both affirms and denies the hard and very real presence of her materials – marble and stone – as she questions continuously her role in the certainties and wonderings of life.

Marble
La Lune d'hiver, 2000 by France Hogué, 50cm x 50cm / 20in x 20in, mixed media, marble.

The French artist France Hogué has been exhibiting her work in Paris and beyond since 1976. She began by studying painting at the Ecole Nationale Supérieure des Beaux Arts in Paris, and teaches mosaic at the Ecole d'Art Americaines de Fontainebleau. The natural world, made up of stones and rocks, inspired the artist to enquire into their true nature by creating an intimate dialogue with the material through the art of mosaic.

MARBLE DUST This can be used in place of sand with white Portland cement, or cement colour, in order to obtain a good mortar and a truer colour.

MARMORINA (also known as Roman Plaster) Crushed marble or marble dust, used in the making of mortars and most often mixed with lime to form a strong adhesive plaster.

MARQUETRY A decorative technique in which the pattern and the ground are smoothed on one plane.

MARQUISE TILES Inlaid stone tiles.

MASKING The protection of an area during the mosaic making processes. It is achieved most often by masking out an area with tape during grouting to avoid affecting another area, which may include the frame.

MASON'S HAMMER A hammer whose wedge-side or cross-peen is used to split along a seam of slate or rock. Use a hammer to chisel a groove along a scored break line, and turn over and hammer gently on the opposite side to secure a break.

MASTIC An organic adhesive from the mastic tree (*Pistacia lentiscus*), used traditionally as a binder. The word is now used as a general term for an adhesive binder, which may be made up of cement, lime, powdered brick or even tar. In present-day Greece it is used mixed with beeswax and paraffin in a ratio of beeswax 100 : paraffin 50 : mastic 5. **See *shellac.***

MATERIALS FOR MOSAIC These are generally hard-wearing and durable, having individual qualities for exploration. They include (i) **stones**: pebbles, stone chips, sandstone, marble, semi-precious (from lapidary suppliers); (ii) **glass**: vitreous mosaic, opaque mosaic, 'classical' mosaic (smalti), stained glass, weathered glass, mirror (iii) **ceramic**: crockery, china, pottery, tiles (glazed and unglazed); (iv) **found objects**: computer parts, etc.

MDF Medium-density fibreboard. This can be used as a backing material for internal work only. Vary the thickness according to the size of mosaic; 12mm / ¹/₂ in thick for up to 1m / 1 yard in area.

MEANDER / MAEANDER A motif used in border patterns where lines meet at right angles and cross each other, often in a continuous pattern of swastika design; also known as a fret or Greek key. **See *cable pattern illustration, page 25.***

MEDIUM The material(s) used by an artist, e.g. mosaic, paint.

METAL There are two kinds: (1) ferrous, which are iron and alloys of iron; and (2) non-ferrous, which include all the others. Gold, silver and platinum are termed 'noble' metals.

METAL CUTTERS Tools used for cutting wire, wire mesh and netting as used in assemblage and constructing on an armature.

METAL-FOIL PAPER Paper-backed foil, found as single sheets or in books. It comes in gold, aluminium, silver, copper and various colours; but be aware of any tarnishing properties.

METAL-LEAF Metal that has been rolled or beaten to an extremely thin sheet, and backed on to glass (gold-leaf glass) or paper, e.g. gold, silver, palladium, aluminium and copper. These are supplied in books protected by finely waxed tissue paper. Similar effects can be achieved by spraying the back of glass – of various kinds – with metallic paints, e.g. gold, aluminium and silver spray paints.

Meander
The Galla Placidia mausoleum, Ravenna Italy, 5th century AD, dedicated to the daughter of Theodosius the Great, is a truly beautiful monument to early Byzantine mosaic decoration. The balance of mosaic and architecture is supreme; the walls, vaults, lunettes and dome are covered in smalti and the interior is dematerialized into a mystical, wondrous chromatism. A hierarchy of Byzantine symbolism is apparent, from symbols of heaven through further symbols of the Evangelists to the Apostles. The souls of humankind are depicted as pairs of doves drinking from a water fountain and a water bowl, to gain eternal life. Decoration abounds on the soffits and vaults, from bands of vines, scrolls, undulating ribbons and rich ornamentation of fruits and flowers, to brilliantly coloured maeanders, some simple and some here involving a swastika pattern of three-dimensional complexity. Here the abaculi glow, enhanced by the alabaster-paned windows.

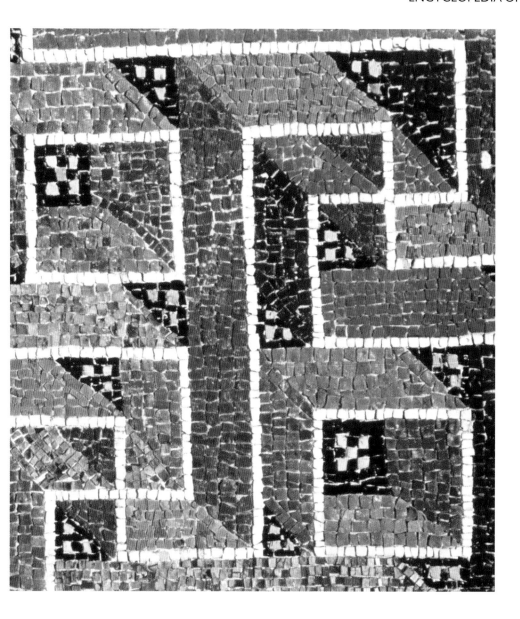

Meander
Homage to Constable, 1991 by Lucio Orsoni, 120cm x 120cm / 48in x 48in, mosaic gold, smalti.

The esteemed Venetian artist, Lucio Orsoni, has evolved a very personal maeander pattern to frame his less abstract works. The rich frame terminating the central grid-like form recalls the trachyte pavement decoration of St Mark's Square in Venice and also makes direct links with early Greco–Roman pavement decoration. This work was made for a show in Leighton House, London, in 1991, in which the Venetian artist collaborated in an exhibition entitled 'The Constructed Image', with the late Niki de St Phalle (France), Susan Bacik (USA) and the author, Elaine M Goodwin (England). The work was made in homage to the great English painter John Constable (1776–1817), and Orsoni's links with England when, as a very young man, he assisted Boris Anrep in the mosaic decoration of Westminster Cathedral, Victoria, London.

METALLIC FOIL To adhere gold and silver leaf or foil to glass, use an acrylic gold size to hold the leaf to the glass to obtain a mirrored effect. **See *water gilding.***

METHODS See *direct; double reverse; indirect.*

MEXICAN MOSAIC There are two types of Mexican mosaic, known as Mixtec or Aztec mosaic. These are mosaics of precious stones such as turquoise, shell, mother of pearl, garnet and lignite, applied to wooden or ivory bases or even skulls, from pre- and post-Columbian America. The term may also include mosaics made from beads and feathers from pre-Columbian days in South and Central America, which were applied to headwear and ceremonial garments.

MEXICAN TILES Low-fired terracotta tiles.

MICRO MOSAIC (It. *mosaico minuto*) Highly detailed work made up of minute tesserae, approx. 500 per sq.cm / 1400 tesserae per sq.in, in the form of jewellery, boxes and pictures, etc. It was very popular during the 18th century, and was bought and collected from Rome and the Vatican City by those on the Grand Tour in Europe. It was originally discovered by chemists at the Vatican mosaic workshop where they developed the matt opaque coloured glass tile material called 'smalti'.

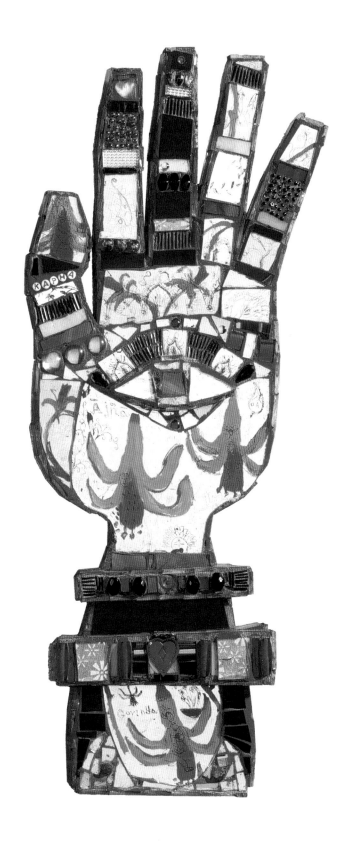

Metallic foil
Ajña, 2002 by David J Hollington, 20cm x 50cm / 8in x 20in, gilded glass, semiprecious stones, found objects.

David J Hollington (b.1964) trained at Central St Martins in London, England, and is a co-founder and member of the Open # Group Collective. His work is inspired by Hindu philosophy and imagery. In this work, the glass used is water gilded with metallic foil and cut into various shapes. The gilded material is then etched and painted over in oil before it is adhered to a wooden base, and the whole mosaic grouted with brilliantly coloured powder pigments.

MILLEFIORI (lit. one thousand flowers) A form of mosaic glass, also known as cane-mosaic, in which circular canes of mosaic glass are arranged in patterns and are sometimes covered with glass. The technique, originating in Egypt, was used for pressed glass bowls and inlay plaques, where an arrangement of coloured glass rods is fused together to make a composite rod, from which transverse slices are cut. A very early and often missed example can be seen in the hair of Dionysos sitting on a panther, 4th century BC, Pella, Greece.

Millefiori

Byzantine Fishermen, 2002 by Martin Cheek, 83 x 81.5cm / 32 ¹/₂in x 32in, smalti, gold mirror, handmade ceramic elements, millefiori.

The British artist Martin Cheek (b. 1959) studied graphic design at Exeter College of Art and Design and worked for many years as a lecturer in animation at the Royal College of Art in London. He sees his mosaic work as a 'logical development from animation', building up through character and movement from many thousands of parts. He continues to experiment and combine a variety of materials in unexpected and often humorous ways. In this work the artist was inspired to emulate the cloisonné effect of the 10th-century Pala d'Oro golden enamelled altar screen in St Mark's, Venice. A combination of materials is used: mosaic smalti, millefiori in the sails, frame and boat decoration, and hand-fired ceramics for the hands and faces, which were glazed with underglaze and finished with gold glaze, producing a highly decorative mosaic assemblage.

MINERAL The general term for granite, quartz, obsidian, lava, etc.

MIRROR MOSAIC Mosaic that uses a preponderance of mirror, a glass that is backed with metal to give an intensely reflective surface. It can be bought in many forms as made-up mirrors, in sheets or in tile form. It is easy to cut using mosaic hand nippers or a glass cutter. Some kinds of mirror on a permanently bound flexible backcloth (mirror flex) are ideal for curved or flat surfaces in any interior setting. Tarnishing may occur in external settings or where humidity gathers, e.g. bathrooms. Mirror may have a variety of finishes and colours, including antiqued and bronzed effects.

MITRE BOX A tool used in the cutting of 45° corners (or others) accurately. It is useful in creating good joints for edging and making up mosaic frames or boxes.

MIXTUM See *opus mixtum.*

MODELLING CLAY / PLASTICINE This pliable building material can be used in the double reverse method of mosaic making and is suitable for mounting stones, pebbles and uneven ceramics, useful since the laying process is not hidden. To set a mosaic into modelling clay, a slab is rolled and laid level on a board, and the tesserae set face up into position. Level the mosaic by covering it with a board and hammering gently. Cover the surface with a damp piece of rough gauze and brush with a watersoluble paste, and leave to dry. Lay a piece of wood on top, turn the whole work over, and peel off modelling clay. Place the mosaic with the gauze in position, using a cement mortar base – be aware of the thickness of tesserae used – and tap level. When the mortar has hardened or set, wash off the gauze with warm water and grout carefully.

MOHS SCALE A system devised by Friedrich Mohs (1773–1839) who classified stones by their degree of hardness – i.e. their ability to withstand being scratched – from the softest to the hardest on a system of 1 : 10.

Soft stones	(1) talc, (2) gypsum
Semi-hard stones	(3) calcite, (4) fluorite, (5) apatite
Hard stones	(6) feldspar, (7) quartz, (8) topaz, (9) corundum, (10) diamond

MONOCHROME Of a single colour; of a mosaic, composed of tesserae in tones of one colour.

MORTAR A mixture consisting of a binder, an aggregate and water – this is normally cement, sand and water – which, when mixed and left in the right conditions (damp), sets hard and resists water and weather, and hardens even under water. **See *plaster; lime putty.***

MOSAIC (Gk. MΩΣAÏKON) A work of art whose surface is composed of individually cut pieces of material coming together to form a whole. The origin of the word is uncertain, but it may have come from the word 'muse' (see below), as the personifications of the Muses were thought to play in grottoes decorated in a mosaic-like manner. Or the word 'mosaic' may have derived from the idea of a wall decoration. The word appears to be a good deal later than the technique. Whatever the case, mosaic is true to itself, is set in concrete, is here to stay, and is at present enjoying a true revival and appreciation.

MOSAIC ART The art of embellishing a surface with a design made of juxtaposed pieces of material, e.g. glass, stone, ceramic – called tesserae, which are

Mirror Mosaic
Jai Mandir, Amber Palace, Jaipur, India, 17th century.

Reflective surfaces that deflect and reflect light have always intrigued mosaicists since ancient times when glass was employed in external nymphaea, and smalti and gold covered the walls of early churches and mosques. A reflective surface plays an enormous part in the mosaic medium, evoking ambiguity, mystery and an intense involvement with all types of light sources. An extreme example is mirror in all its shapes, forms and application. This room of the palace at Amber is an exquisite example of the power and beauty of mirror mosaic. Each mirror tessera is slightly curved to catch and throw light around the room. A single candle would create myriad light reflections like a star-lit sky. Much of the surface design is abstract, with interspersed patterns of a still life – vases and beautifully formed vessels. Note too, in this damaged example, the under-painting, like a sinope, for guidance.

fixed to the surface with an adhesive binder and used in walls, floors and on other architectural planes or as portable panels. The individual units of material are anonymous in themselves (i.e. they need have no definable shape) but when put together they create a homogeneous design. This may be decorative, abstract, illustrative or geometric, and of two- or three-dimensional aspect.

MOSAIC CUTTERS / NIPPERS / CLIPPERS / PINCERS (It. *tenaglia*) The main cutting tool for mosaicists. It is used primarily for cutting glass and ceramic. There are several types:

1. A spring-loaded mosaic cutter with tungsten carbide tips. There are two versions, standard and longer-handled to give good leverage. These are also known as spring-type Japanese nippers.

2. An 'American' cutter, spring-loaded, with carbide cutting wheels, which is excellent for cutting long, oblong shapes. The carbide wheel can be adjusted with an accompanying key to move the wheel around as the cutting edge begins to wear.

3. An adjustable cutter able to accommodate different thicknesses by adjusting a screw, and with special hardened cutting edges and a spring joint. A freestanding table-mounted universal mosaic cutter has been developed for cutting both stone and glass, and is a useful alternative to hand-held nippers. It has steel blades that may be sharpened. **See *cutters*.**

MOSAIC GLASS An object made from pre-formed glass elements, placed in a mould and heated to fuse together. It is also the generic term for glass tesserae used in mosaic making.

MOSAICIST A mosaic maker or creator of mosaics; cf. sculptor, painter.

MOSAIC MURAL A mosaic that is executed, *in situ*, on a wall internally or externally, generally of large size. The term (in modern usage) frequently refers to mosaics in playgrounds, communities and car parks, etc., and may involve a group of artists or participants.

Mosaic cutters – (a) spring-loaded
These spring-loaded cutters are the most commonly used by mosaicists today and are ideal for cutting ceramic, glass and china tesserae. The handles of the cutter are held well down in the cutting hand to give greater leverage. The material to be cut is introduced, just a little, into the jaw of the cutter with the other hand and held in position with the thumb and middle finger opposite the direction of the line to be cut. The legs of the cutter are squeezed as the material is firmly held, and a clean, straight fracture is made. (JM)

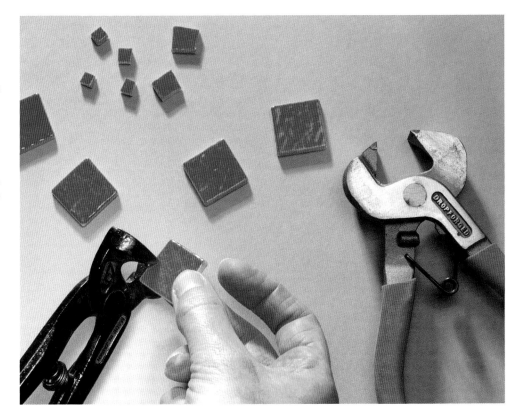

Mosaic cutters – (b) carbide wheel mosaic cutter
These cutters have cutting wheels that can be adjusted by an accompanying key when they become blunted. They are excellent for cutting strips of material, including mirror and stained and vitreous glass. The material is introduced into the centre of the jaw of the cutter – a different angle from (a) above – and again the material is held, with some pressure, opposite the intended line of fracture. (JM)

Mosaic cutters – (c) adjustable
This cutter is a personal favourite, popular from the mid-20th century and still available. It is a spring-loaded cutter with adjustable jaws, to adapt to materials of different thickness. The cutting principle is the same as in (a), and the fracture is effected cleanly and very accurately, with very little effort. (JM)

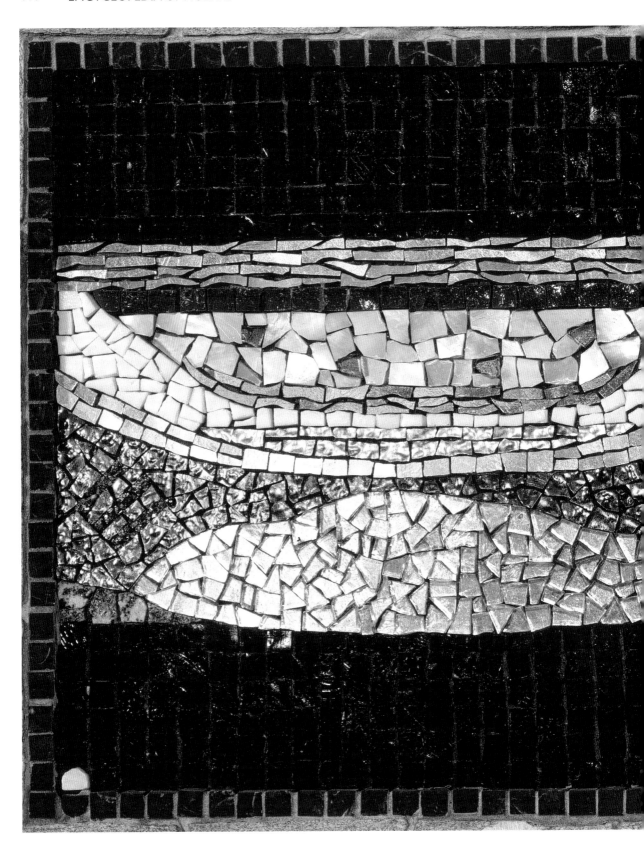

MOSAIC NIPPERS See *mosaic cutters.*

MOSAIC PLAQUE A wall-hung decoration. Made from the 1st century AD onwards, it consists of a matrix or binding agent with various opaque coloured inlays.

MOSAIC SCULPTURE See *sculptural mosaics.*

MOTHER OF PEARL An iridescent lining of mollusc shells, e.g. pearl oyster. The alternative layers of calcium carbonate and conchiolin are generally cut with a hacksaw. Mother of pearl was first used in mosaic in the early Byzantine period, with examples seen in the mosaics of Theodora and Justinian in San Vitale, Ravenna, Italy (early 6th century), and the Great Mosque of Damascus, Syria (8th century), and later in the 11th century monastery of Daphni, Greece, where the female saint Anastasia has only one mother of pearl earring!

Mother of pearl
Reflecting Gold II, 1999 by Elaine M Goodwin, 30cm x 30cm / 12in x 12in, smalti antico, Venetian gold/silver leaf, granite, mother of pearl. (Private collection.) (JM)

The author, the artist Elaine M Goodwin, spent her early childhood in the islands of Hong Kong and recalls a fixation with watching the small native boats, *sampan,* each carrying coloured lanterns, move over the water at night. Light and its enigmatic quality continues to be explored in her work. In this piece, one of contemplation, it is the more muted light-diffusing surfaces of antique smalti and the nacreous quality of mother of pearl, taken from very large Pacific shells once collected by and belonging to Boris Anrep, that enhance the mood of the work.

MULTIPLE DECOR A design based on a grid, containing many small panels of widely differing designs (see right).

MUSAEUM (pl. **musaea**) A room or building for the Muses; dedicated to art and study, and inspiration, from which our word museum derives. **See *museum*.**

MUSE (Gk. MOYΣA – a muse) There were nine Muses – daughters of Zeus and Mnemosyne – who were patrons of the arts and inspirers of artists: Clio, Euterpe, Thalia, Melpomene, Terpsichore, Erato, Polyhymnia, Urania and Calliope.

MUSEIARIUS / MUSEARIUS / MUSIVARIUS (pl. **musivarii**) A classical term for one who specializes in *opus musivum* i.e. making wall mosaics. It also refers to a mosaic worker, a mosaicist, a craftsman in *opus musivum* or in mosaic work in general.

MUSEUM Pertaining to the Muses; the mosaicist's art form may have taken its name from grottoes sacred to the nymphs or the Muses; many Roman grottoes were decorated with mosaics of shells, stones and glass paste. An inspiring conjecture!

MUSIVUM A word referring to a wall mosaic or a vault mosaic. **See *opus musivum*.**

Multiple decor
A Moment in Time in Exeter (Millennium Mosaic), 2000, created by people in Exeter, England, 670cm × 275cm / 22ft × 9ft. (JM)

This mural in the centre of the Guildhall precinct in the City of Exeter was designed by Garry Plastow and Sam Watts and made by the citizens of Exeter, and can be seen as an example of multiple decor technique. Each person or group of persons was given a tile of identical and regular dimensions, and in the spirit of prospect for the 3rd Millennium created a design accordingly. Some designs were painted directly on to the tile, others had textural finishes and some were constructed as a mosaic. The tiles were then assembled to create a uniform whole.

NAÏVE MOSAIC Mosaic produced by self-taught or untutored creators, where the motivation 'to make' is to the fore. Such mosaics are often of great ingenuity and large vision, and have a tendency to use recycled or scrap materials, often with much innate ability.

NATURAL MATERIALS If these are durable, many can be used for mosaic work; e.g. stone, marble, semiprecious and precious stones, mother of pearl, clay, pebbles, shells, slate, feathers, etc.

NEUTRAL Of no particular colour. Generically used to mean muted or of modified colouring.

NIBBLING Gently cutting away at glass, with pliers or mosaic nippers; for example, when smoothing the edges of a circle or other particular shape. **See parrot nibblers; cutters.**

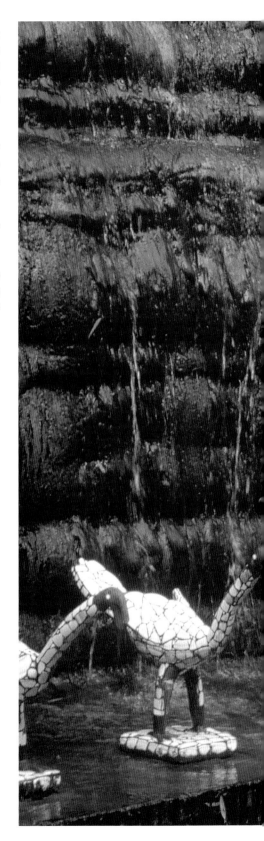

Naïve mosaic
The Rock Garden (detail), 2000 by Nek Chand Saini, Chandigarh, India, approx. 30 hectares, recycled materials, miscellaneous. (EMG)

Nek Chand Saini (born c. 1924) is a living legend. As a young man in Karachi, he dreamt of creating a kingdom in which to sit and contemplate. In the 1950s he and his new wife Kamla began to realize his vision in Chandigarh, the new Punjabi city of the French architect Le Corbusier – a city constructed as sectors in a grid-like system. In secret and hidden from public gaze, using the debris of modern city life – crockery, sanitary ware, porcelain light fittings, neon light tubes, bangles, bottle tops, etc. – the kingdom began to materialize. Water carriers, dancing bears, camels, elephants, school children, dancers, warriors and many more three-dimensional birds, animals and people were created as sculptures with armatures of iron, covered in cement-soaked rags and sacking. Now, in 2003, after the author's return visit to pay homage to the man and his kingdom (Elaine M Goodwin had the great privilege of working in the Rock Garden during the 1980s), the final Phase Three of the Kingdom is nearing completion, and is resplendent with waterfalls, palaces, and an open area with an arena and 50 swings to welcome the many thousands of local and international visitors who come to see the garden daily. Nek Chand's vision is enjoyed by all, and by the man himself – he remains a man of enormous innovation, humility and a deep dignity.

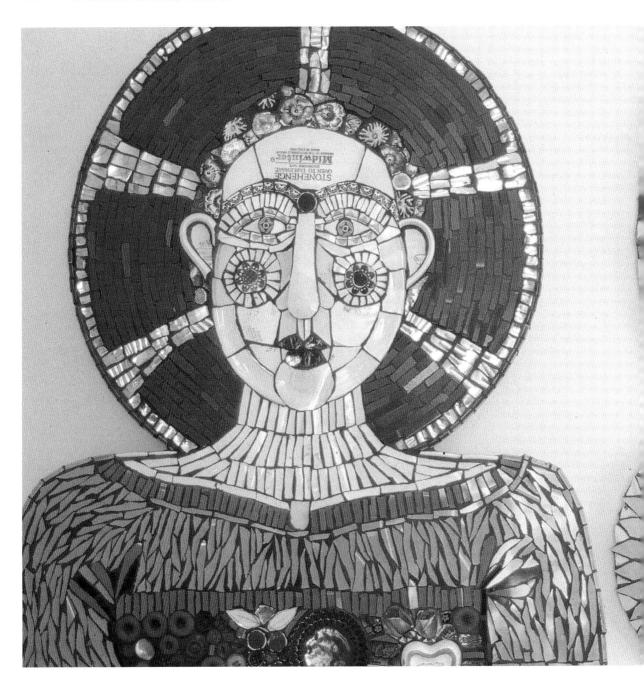

NIMBUS (pl. **nimbi**) An aureole, halo, or the disc of light surrounding a head, usually of a saint or deity. When a square (instead of a circle) is seen behind the head of a person in religious mosaics, it denotes that they were still alive when the mosaic was being made (e.g. Teodora, the mother of Pope Pasqualis I, seen in a detail from the early 9th-century apse mosaic in the chapel of St Zeno in S. Prassede, Rome, Italy).

NON-REPRESENTATIONAL A work of art (including a mosaic) not representing the natural or the real in any way. See *abstract.*

NOTCHED TROWEL A trowel used to spread the mortar of a setting bed before laying a mosaic. The tool leaves a textured surface for greater adherence. It generally has a 3mm x 3mm / ^{1}/8in x ^{1}/8in gauge to give the correct setting depth and prevent the cement from seeping up through the tiles. See *float.*

NUCLEUS The traditional name given to the upper layer of mortar in the bedding for a pavement mosaic. See *emblema* **diagram,** page 52.

NUGGETS See *globs.*

NYMPH A female spirit inhabiting the water, sea or woods, etc. A sea nymph can also be known as a nereid.

NYMPHAEUM (pl. **nymphaea**) A grotto containing a decorative fountain, with a running water source dedicated to the nymphs and inhabited by them or the Muses. It may also be called a '*musaeum*'. Both the early classical Roman nymphaea, which were natural, and the later 16th- and 17th-century artificial grottoes, e.g. the 16th-century Boboli Gardens in Florence Italy, used shells, including mussel shells, pumice, marble chips and mosaic glass to great decorative effect.

Nimbus
Sun Figure + the Crowd (detail, *Brother Sun*), 2002 by Cleo Mussi, life-sized: china, crockery, platters.

British artist Cleo Mussi trained in textiles at Goldsmith's College of Art in London, where she was a contemporary of the artist Damien Hirst. Her work is known for its lively innovation in working with recycled china and tiles. Self-taught, the artist is able to explore the mosaic medium without traditional restraints. In this mosaic the life-sized standing figure has been deified with a nimbus of brilliant vermilion. Humour, texture and colour abound – and the viewer can be rewarded by inner stirrings that touch on a very real hidden primordial response!

OECUS (pl. **oeci**) A large reception room in a Hellenistic or Roman house, often richly decorated with floor mosaics.

OFFICINA (L.; pl. **officinae**) Term for a workshop in which mosaic work is carried out. For example, in 4th-century AD Britain there were at least four distinctive officinae, probably based at Dorchester (Durnovaria), Cirencester (Corinium), Water Newton (Durobrivae) in Cambridgeshire and Brough-on-Humber (Petuaria). Each officina had a range of motifs, some unique and some crossovers, but always with variation in the quality of work. A modern mosaic workshop is that at Spilimbergo (Italy), founded in 1922 and known as the 'Scuola Mosaicisti del Friuli', which runs a three-year course in cutting techniques, materials, design and facsimile, but also encourages innovative and original work.

OGEE (adj. **Ogival**) A shape formed by back-to-back curves, one concave and one convex; therefore double curved.

OIL PUTTY An excellent plaster for fixing non-porous tesserae, such as glass and gold tesserae. Mix 60% powdered travertine and 25% slaked lime with 10% raw or crude linseed oil and 5% boiled linseed oil to make a very malleable plaster that will keep its plasticity for up to two weeks in dry, temperate conditions and then dry hard without shrinkage.

ONYX A semiprecious stone that is a transparent variety of quartz. It is often banded in gently shaded variations, from white to red to black. **See *stones.***

OPAQUE Not transparent: referring, for example, to types of glass or other mosaic material.

OPIFICIO Italian, from the Latin *opificium*, workshop. One well-known opificio is the Grand Ducal Workshop of Pietre Dure; begun in 1580 in the Casino of San Marco, Italy, it is now a training school for producing pietre-dure work. **See *pietre dure.***

OPTICAL MIXING The mixing of colours on the mosaic surface by the eye. The colours are individual units of tesserae that, when juxtaposed and seen from a distance, form another colour; for example, red/blue = purple. **See *juxtaposition; secondary colours.***

OPUS (pl. **opera**; lit. work) A term used mainly by modern writers, following the lead of the elder Pliny, to describe various mosaic tessellation techniques and brickwork constructions and patterning (not all ancient). It is useful to be aware of how each opus affects the look of the surface by giving a different 'weight' or 'feel' to the mosaic. There is sometimes confusion or difference of opinion as to exactly what is meant by the names of some opus designs!

OPUS AFRICANUM A masonry style, common in North Africa, in which a framework of stone made of horizontals and verticals is filled in with small stones or rubble.

OPUS ALEXANDRINUM Originally the style used for an *opus sectile* floor, using red porphyry and green serpentine, it can now be used to mean a floor mosaic, generally in black and white on a reddish/pinkish background.

OPUS CAEMENTICIUM ('mortared rubble') Roman concrete, which consists of rubble aggregate laid in a lime mortar. Fragments of stone, brick and aggregate are laid in a mortar of lime, sand and pozzolana. Also 'petit appareil' in Roman Gaul, which used small squared blocks that followed a regular coursing.

OPUS FIGLINUM A pavement formed from squares of pottery, tile or terracotta set flat or on edge forming a herringbone-like pattern. It is also used to mean oblong tesserae in pairs or threes laid to create a woven effect. *Opus figlinum* was used in the 2nd and 1st century BC, where oblong or rectangular-shaped tesserae in marble, stone or terracotta were sometimes combined with a cube of a different colour, e.g. Morgantina, Sicily.

OPUS INCERTUM A masonry technique using small stones or rubble, thus forming a mosaic made up of irregularly cut tesserae.

OPUS INTERRASILE A marble slab, usually whole, with areas chiselled out to a depth of around

Onyx
Lamento, 1985 by
Fabrice Vannier, 170cm
x 100cm / 67in x 39in,
onyx, travertine,
marble, limestone,
slate, granite, wood.

The French artist
Fabrice Vannier (b.
1963) lives and works
in Paris. He studied
antique mosaic art in
France at the
Sorbonne, Paris, and
also in Barcelona, Spain,
where he practised
painting, engraving and
mosaic. A true
mosaicist, his
inspiration arises from
the poetry and
mythology associated
with the
Mediterranean.

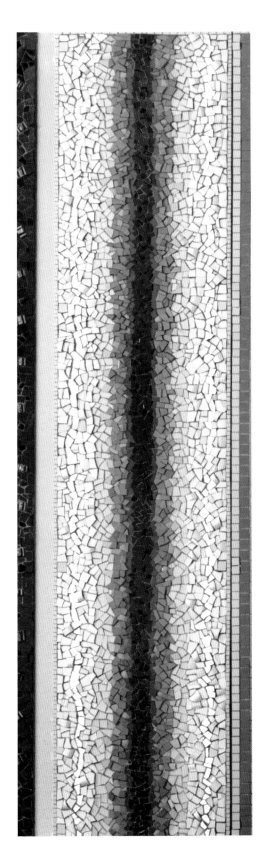

Opus palladianum
Opus panel (i), 1999, Elaine M Goodwin and Group 5,
50cm x 153cm / 20in x 60in, ceramic, mirror, glass. (JM)

One of a number of panels made for the exhibition
Mosaic — A Living Art: An Anglo-Italian Celebration at the
Royal Albert Memorial Museum and Art Gallery in
Exeter, England, 2000. This panel of opus palladianum
creates an intricate surface of carefully tessellated
tesserae of very irregular shape but similar size. Its
impact in this case is due to the merging of one
material with another, for example, the mirror lines
with the adjoining glass tesserae.

1cm / $^3/_8$ in to receive polychrome geometric tesserae. The slab is then polished smooth.

OPUS LATERICIUM (lit. 'wall work') A type of brickwork; a brick wall containing a circular ornament made up of brick tiles, e.g. at Pompeii, 1st century AD, Italy.

OPUS MIXTUM (lit. 'mixed work') A type of masonry combining brickwork and areas of *opus reticulatum*, seen as a wall facing of reticulate or net-structured masonry with levelling courses and quoins of brick.

OPUS MUSIVUM The work of the Muses, i.e. mosaic. The term is originally thought to have been used to refer to wall and vault work. It is also a term referring to the decorating of nymphaea or 'musaea', with shells, pumice, marble, glass, etc. It was later understood by some historians to refer to the entire mosaic where *opus tessellatum* and *opus vermiculatum* combine to form a homogeneous floor covering. As a technique, it originally denoted a cartoon used as a guide that was sketched on to the penultimate layer of wall plaster. A master craftsman or musivarius would work on the figure and the face and the assistants would do the rest and the background; each artist adding a final layer of plaster to a small section and laying the tesserae accordingly. **See carpet pattern.**

OPUS PALLADIANA / PALLADIANUM A paving or background to a mosaic that is composed of random and irregularly shaped tesserae that are, however, carefully tessellated. It is a modern term and used in modern mosaic making, especially for awkward 'fill-in' shapes. It is sometimes called crazy paving mosaic.

OPUS PAVIMENTUM A form of *opus sectile* deployed in a chequered pattern. **See opus quadratum.**

OPUS QUADRATUM Squared stone masonry, a building technique used in the Roman Republican period.

OPUS REGULATUM / QUASI REGULATUM A technique in which the stones or tesserae are placed very regularly like a computer design or diagonally set as in a net-like pattern.

OPUS RETICULATUM (lit. 'network') Small blocks set diagonally or in very regular rows of horizontal and vertical lines. It is a type of masonry consisting of a concrete core faced with pyramidal stones set so the bases show a regular network on the exposed face. It may also mean a wall of small polygonal tuff (*tufa*) bricks, set in mortar in fairly regular rows.

OPUS ROMANUM A term for Roman floor decoration composed of rare marble and glass tesserae, used in decorative bands and geometric designs. **See cosmatesque.**

OPUS SCUTULATUM (L. *scutulae*, 'lozenges') This term is generally applied (1) to pieces of marble tesserae in a floor, e.g. coloured random pieces set into an otherwise fairly regular marble tessellated floor. It may also mean (2) floors paved with cubic patterns shown in perspective, i.e. cubes or lozenge-shaped pieces depicted in a 3D fashion; often made of juxtaposed coloured marbles, slate and green limestone lozenge shapes, e.g. pavements in the House of the Faun, Pompeii, Italy, 1st century AD.

OPUS SECTILE (lit. 'cut work') A decorative floor paving or wall covering using multicoloured stone, marble or tile cut into thin slabs of geometric shapes. It is therefore a surface decoration using specific geometric or other shapes of interlocking marble or stone inlay, being in effect a form of marquetry.

OPUS SEGMENTATUM A floor covering made of many coloured marbles in figurative or geometric shapes – perhaps a forerunner of modern-day terrazzo work.

OPUS SIGNINUM From Signia (modern Segni), an Italian town known for its red clay. It is a waterproof wall or floor lining of crushed red brick or pottery, with chips of marble or terracotta. It was often used in ancient times in pools and cisterns.

OPUS SPICATUM Stone or marble tesserae laid in a herringbone pattern, or like a wheat ear (*spica*).

Opus tessellatum

Opus panel (ii), 1999,
Elaine M Goodwin and
Group 5, 60cm x 153cm /
24in x 60in, ceramic,
mirror, vitreous glass. (JM)

The second of a series of
panels, designed as
sample panels to show
the varying techniques
displayed in modern
mosaic making, and made
for the previously
mentioned Anglo–Italian
exhibition, paying
homage to a very ancient
way of laying tesserae, in
regular rows, and with
regular cube-like units of
material. The very
regulated patterning
gives a very strong, even
monumental feel to the
panel.

Opus vermiculatum

Opus panel (iii), 1999,
Elaine M Goodwin and
Group 5, 60cm x 153cm /
24in x 60in, ceramic,
vitreous glass, mirror. (JM)

The third in a series of
sample panels (see
above) displaying how
the opus techniques of
placing tessera may be
used to create widely
differing surfaces in
mosaic. The placing of
the tesserae in
exaggerated and
elongated curves
creates a strong
dynamic and tension on
the mosaic surface, and
demonstrates clearly
that by studying and
understanding the
classical and ancient
techniques of brick and
tesserae construction
and laying, modern
mosaicists can explore
and adapt the
techniques for their
own use to create
textural and interesting
visual effects.

OPUS TESSELLATUM Originally a term for floor mosaics, this is now a generic term for all mosaic pavements made of cut and tessellated pieces called tesserae, usually cubes of approx. 5mm ($^3/_{16}$in) and over. The term may also refer to a way of laying backgrounds or areas of mosaic in fairly regular horizontal or vertical lines to give the image a feeling of fixture or stasis.

OPUS TESTACEUM A Roman wall-facing of brick or tiles set fairly regularly in mortar.

OPUS VERMICULATUM A style in which the tesserae, sometimes irregularly shaped, are laid in a 'wormlike' fashion. They are usually composed of smaller cubes and are used to articulate specific areas within the design. Originally, in Hellenic times, it was a technique deploying minute tesserae in small curves within a mosaic, and often following tonal variation. Today the tesserae are of any size, and are used to create movement, either within an image or in a background.

ORNAMENTAL COMPOSITION A decorative composition relying for its aesthetic value on the power of patterning or design. An ornamental mosaic is one with a pronounced decorative arrangement. See *arabesques; decorative mosaic; design elements.*

OUTSIDER ART Mosaic that is untutored and naïve in the extreme – sometimes with little aesthetic value but compulsive in motivation and often a *tour de force.*

Outsider art
Fantasy Garden, Viry Noureuil, France, 1940s–present by Bodan Litnanski (seen here), miscellaneous. (EMG)

The Russian-born creator extraordinaire Bodan Litnanski (born c. 1915) was repatriated in France after World War II, where he found a dilapidated house which he has rebuilt to his fantasy vision. House-front, retaining walls, garden and pathways are covered in a fantastical arrangement of scrap materials. Some more traditional mosaic materials such as discarded shells and pebbles have semblances of patterning and underlying beauty of form. All else is an extraordinary assemblage of stones, pots, car parts, dolls, garden ware and scrap and found objects combined in unique and bizarre architectural and decorative arrangements. The garden is always open, and the creator continues to add to his environment and is more than delighted to welcome visitors.

P

PALAEOLOGAN AGE   The last period of the Byzantine age, from the 13th to mid-15th century, which saw a further flowering of mosaic art.

PALAIOLOGOS (pl. **Palaiologoi**)   The last of the Byzantine Emperors, 1261–1461, beginning with Michael VIII Palaiologos.

PALETTE   The selection or range of colours used in a mosaic.

PALETTE KNIFE   A flexible, usually metal-ended tool, with a wooden handle, that can be used in mosaic making for grouting or for spreading adhesive, etc.

PALMETTE   A decorative motif in the form of a stylized palm-leaf, often seen in Classical pavements, etc., as an ornament composed of simple leaves arranged in a fan shape, e.g. in the pebble mosaic borders at Pella, Greece, 4th century BC.

PALOMBINO (lit. 'dove-coloured')   A grey-white, fine-grained limestone used in *opus sectile*.

PANTOCRATOR   Meaning all-powerful or almighty, an epithet applied to an image of Christ, often enthroned and holding a book in his left hand and making a gesture of benediction with his right hand. Depictions can be seen in the apses or cupolas of churches and monasteries, e.g. in Cefalù, Sicily, 12th century.

PAPER CUT-OUTS   Multiple shapes created from folded paper used as an aid when needing repeat motifs in a design.

PAPER MOSAIC   A form of mosaic using torn or cut pieces of paper. It is usual to observe two rules: no overlapping and no touching of the paper tesserae. This is often a good way to learn the rudiments of mosaic making, particularly for young children.

PARISON (from Fr. *paraison*, 'preparation')   A gather of slightly inflated glass on the end of a blowpipe in glassmaking.

PARROT NIBBLERS   A springloaded mosaic cutter with small jaws that are good for intricate shaping, e.g. concave and convex 'nibbling'. **See *nibbling*.**

PARTING AGENT   A substance that is brushed, rubbed or sprayed onto a frame, mould or wooden shuttering that stops concrete or cement from sticking to it. This may be wax, petroleum jelly, etc. **See *release agent; vaseline.***

PATENT MOSAIC   These are dust-pressed tiles, with mosaic markings pressed into the surface. When these indents are cement-filled, the mosaic impressions give the illusion of 'true' mosaic, but at a fraction of the time and cost.

PATIR (Persian)   A flowing ribbon associated with Royal glory, often tied around the neck of a bird (in the Zoroastrian religion, birds protect mankind from evil). As an intercultural transfer it can be seen in mosaics from Jordan, at Umm al-Rasas, south-east of Madaba, Jordan, late 6th century.

PATTERN BOOKS   Collections of patterns, motifs and designs, as used by mosaicists. In Roman times, they are believed to have featured a selection of designs, individual motifs and decorations that were often retained or repeated to give consistency from one century to another, and that were typical of a region. When they were imported, individual variations appeared and interesting diversities occurred among tried and tested motifs. They are used today as transfers in mosaic teaching books and manuals, encouraging copying. **See *copy books; repertory.***

PAVONAZZETTO ('peacock')   A white marble with purple veining from Dokimeion in Phrygia, Turkey.

PEBBLE MOSAICS   The earliest-known are 8th century BC at Gordium in Asia Minor. Fine ancient examples also exist at Eretria, Olynthos and Pella in Greece, 4th and 5th century BC. Pebble mosaics continue to be a popular art form for domestic and civic pavements. Collected pebbles should be sorted and stored according to shape, size and colour, and used alone or with other mosaic materials. **See *lapilli.***

PEBBLES   These are small stones and can be defined by their form: longs or skimmers, which are thin-shaped and used for definition (to add curve) and direction (to add flow); cylinders, which are 'roundish' shaped and therefore non-directional;

Pebble mosaic
Spiral, c. 2000 by Mark Davidson, 2m x 2m / 78in x 78in, pebbles.

The New Zealand artist Mark Davidson (b. 1956) worked as a stained-glass artist for 15 years before being 'smitten' by the ancient and Byzantine mosaics of Rome during a period of international travel in the mid-1990s. A student of the author, Elaine M Goodwin, and of British pebble artist Maggy Howarth, the artist returned to New Zealand in the year 2000, where he has been producing exterior pebble mosaics and teaching the techniques to the present time. This work, with its restraint of colour and design, continues an enquiry into practical, geometric floor design begun so many years earlier in 5th-century Greece.

Photorealism
Try and Try Again! (detail), 1994 by Oliver Budd, Pontypool, Wales, 40 sq. metres /
approx. 45 sq. yards, smalti, ceramic tile, limestone aggregates.

The mosaicist Oliver Budd joined his father's firm in 1982, and trained for five years
under Kenneth Budd's guidance. Since his father's death in 1995, Oliver has carried
on working in the company, continuing the traditions and adding more technical
virtuosity to the firm's output. This mosaic, a rugby football mural featuring
portraits of known and loved players, was set directly on to mesh using a flexible
cement adhesive. The finished panels were fixed at site using explosive bolts.
Aggregates of local Caerphilly stone were set around the mosaic areas directly into
a cement and sand screed.

flat tops, stones that have flat areas and can be slender or round; and quarry stones, which are mixed broken stones. Pebbles must be hard and durable, e.g. granite, slate, jasper, dolerite, syenite, hard limestone, sandstone, quartz, flint and chert. Apart from in the ancient Greek and Mediterranean cultures, pebbles have been used world-wide for greater or lesser symbolic content. In China, garden pebbles are thought of as a microcosm of the larger world and have great symbolic value and balance; the *yin* are dark pebbles (feminine), and the *yang* are bright pebbles (masculine). In the classic Chinese garden, the ground is hammered flat and covered with about 5mm / $^{1}/_{3}$ in of sifted earth into which the patterns are laid. Geometric shapes are delineated by cut strips and carefully selected pebbles of four colours are laid in varying directions. Apart from geometric pebble carpets, flora and fauna are occasionally introduced. A Moorish tradition of pebble laying, seen even today in Andalucia in Spain, has spread to Portugal. Examples exist in many cities in the Algarve, Portugal, e.g. in Vila Real de S. Antonio. There was also a revival of interest during the Renaissance period in the 15th and 16th century, which had an influence in Northern Europe.

PELTA (pl. **peltae**) A lightweight shield carried for instance by Amazons (mythical female warriors). Many Greek and Roman mosaic pavements used the form of a shield as a decorative crescent-shaped motif, with the inner arc replaced by two smaller crescents; it thus has three points, not two. **See *cable pattern illustration, page 25.***

PEPLOS (pl. **peploi**) A woman's tunic, seen on Roman mosaic female figures, secured at the shoulder and falling in folds, with an overhang over the belt at the front and back.

PHOTOREALISM A method favoured by some mosaicists, particularly in the field of portraiture. A colour or black-and-white photo or digital print is used as a template to create the mosaic. At its best an intriguing interpretation of the 'real' is ensured; at its worst a lifeless 'mosaic by numbers' is made.

PIASTRINA (pl. **piastrine**) A form of glass smalti, about 4–5mm / $^{3}/_{16}$ in thick, with a smoothed surface and base. It is used with its flat surface uppermost, unlike traditional smalti where the cut surface is generally the exposed surface to give maximum light refraction. It generally comes in sizes 10 x 10mm and 20 x 20mm / approx. $^{1}/_{2}$–$^{3}/_{4}$ in.

PICASSIETTE This was originally the nickname given to Raymond Isidore (1900–64) of Chartres, in northern France. The pun on the word *picassiette* meant both 'plate-stealer' and 'Picasso of plates', in reference to his home, which he built and decorated completely throughout with found and collected china for over 25 years. The term now loosely refers to mosaic work made of recycled and broken china and tiles. It is also known as pique-assiette, shard-ware and memory ware.

PICTOR IMAGINARIUS (pl. **pictores imaginarii**) A Latin term for the leading mosaic artist, who drew the cartoon (*imago*) and the main features and oversaw the whole work, and was therefore both a specialist painter and designer, particularly of figurative mosaics.

PIETRE DURE (lit. 'hard stones') Florentine hard-stone mosaics of the 16th to 19th century, composed largely of silicates, unlike soft stone marbles and limestones, which are made largely of calcium. The designs are usually made from marbles, minerals and rare semiprecious stones, which are cross cut into 3–6mm / $^{1}/_{8}$–$^{1}/_{4}$in sections called *formelle*, with a small saw or copper wire sharpened by wetted emery. They are then polished smooth. Designs can range from intricate floral patterns to sentimental landscapes. **See *opificio*.**

PIGMENTED PLASTER Early on in Roman Republican times, plaster bedding was frequently coloured blue, red, yellow or green. For example, the Nymphaeum in the House of the Golden Bracelet (Casa del bracciale d'oro), Pompeii, Italy, has rows of shells on a red-coloured stucco (probably a mix of *murex* and cardium).

PIGMENTS Colours obtained from natural sources, such as earth and rocks, e.g. ochres, umbers, siennas, and 'burnt' earth (where the raw pigment is roasted to give a reddish-brown colour). Lime-proof pigments come in a much wider variety of colours, e.g. Cadmium vermilion, red, red deep and brown; Cobalt violet, blue and turquoise; Cerulean

blue, Ultramarine limewash; Chromium oxide; Red, golden and yellow ochre; Indian red; Mars red and violet; Venetian red; Green earth light; Burnt green earth; Terre verte; and Raw umber, all unbleached by the lime in cement. Lustre pigments can also be used – experiment with amounts and ratios by making samplers. **See *artists' pigments; cement pigment*.**

Picassiette
La Maison Picassiette, detail, by Raymond Isidore, 1938–64, rue du Repos, Chartres, France: glass, china, pebbles, stones, tiles, miscellaneous. (EMG)

The Maison Picassiette has given its name to a style of mosaic work that is very popular among modern-day mosaicists, particularly in the USA. The materials are often recycled, and consist mainly of china, tiles and crockery. Raymond Isidore was untutored as an artist; his motivation was inspired by his faith and living in the cathedral city of Chartres with its soaring spires, a motif repeated again and again in his work. What began as an initial desire to decorate his self-built home grew into an obsession to completely cover all the surfaces with mosaic, including his bed, tables, sewing machine, wheelbarrow, and all the walls. It remains a charming testament to himself and his wife and is now a national treasure.

'Pizza' – Venetian smalto
A selection of white tesserae cut from a pizza of smalto, showing the slightly curved edge of the slab, a few chunks cut after the initial scoring, and a group of regular-sized tesserae. These last are an unchanged traditional size, tried and tested since Byzantine times; they are large enough to hold their own in a mosaic as individual units of texture and colour, but small enough to merge in an optical mix when juxtaposed with other colours and viewed from a distance. Note the bubbles and imperfections, and the brilliance of the cut surface. Imperfections such as discoloration or air bubbles add to the rich, 'living' quality of this unique and unsurpassable material. (JM)

PILA (pl. **pilae**) Small pillars of brick or stone forming one part of a hypocaust floor-heating system in Roman buildings and baths.

PIXELLATION This is when the surface of a mosaic is composed of equal-sized, individually coloured tesserae that seem to be randomly placed but form a composite image or design when viewed from a required distance, like the pixels of light in a screened computer image.

'PIZZA' (pl. **'pizze'**) The name given to a disc approx. 1–2cm / $^1/_4$–$^3/_4$ in thick of Venetian glass mosaic or smalti, made from pressing the molten mass of glass, metal oxides and colouring agents. Sometimes the disc is not rounded but oblong in shape, with curved corners. It is from the cooled and hardened 'pizze' that smalti are cut. First they are scored horizontally and vertically with a diamond-pointed tool and cut into chunks of glass, 3–5cm / 1–2in wide, from which smaller and more regular tesserae are cut, approx. 1.5–2 x 1cm / $^3/_8$–$^3/_4$ x $^1/_4$in. The cut edge is turned to the viewer, its reflecting quality being quite brilliant, emphasized by any unevenness in its hand-cut surface. Other terms for the glass disc are pancake, flat disc, slab, strip, plate and piastra.

PLASTER In mosaic this implies a binder or wall-coating, normally made either of cement, sand, plasticizer or lime putty, and water. **See *lime putty; mortar.***

PLASTERBOARD As a base support this is used dry and primed for working on interior mosaics.

PLASTER CAST Sometimes made for 3D mosaics as a maquette for the real thing, to aid in choosing colours, areas of direction or undulations, etc. It is useful because it can be the same size as the finished mosaic and is cheap to make up and colour, using pigment or paint.

PLASTER OF PARIS A gypsum plaster which, when mixed with water, dries solid and is used for casting.

PLASTICIZER A ready-made proprietary liquid, used as an additive in place of hydrated lime in the making of mortar. It aids malleability, retards the drying or curing time, and helps prevent the shrinkage and cracking of mortar when setting.

PLEXIGLASS / PERSPEX Plastic sheets that may be used as a support or lightweight backing material. It allows light to filter through areas of the mosaic. It is weather resistant and can therefore be used in windows and doors, etc.

PLIERS There are various types, useful for holding, grazing and breaking materials in mosaic making.

PLYWOOD A type of timber made from many layers of wood sheets glued together and forming a hard-surfaced wood ideal for mosaic making. There are three types of quality: (1) marine which has resinated layers, and is the heaviest and most expensive; (2) exterior quality/grade; and (3) ordinary quality plywood. The edges are the most vulnerable part of the wood and should be sealed with silicone or other sealers if left exposed.

POINTILLISM A technique used in mosaic and known from painting, involving an optical mixing of colour, e.g. green, made up of blue/yellow. It involves building up colours out of dots of complementary colours, as instinctively known by Byzantine mosaicists, and only scientifically and systematically understood more than twelve hundred years later by Georges Seurat, (1859–91), the French artist whose work was given this name. See *divisionism; juxtaposition.*

POLISHING Occasionally mosaic will benefit by having its surface buffed with a soft dry cloth or rag. Soft cotton or cotton interlock is ideal for this purpose.

POLYSTYRENE FOAM A lightweight material that can be cut to any shape and used as a backing support for three-dimensional mosaics. Cement can be used to build up the form over a cement slurry applied directly to the foam.

PONTIL A solid rod applied to the base of a china object, tile, glass, etc. during its making, which leaves a ring mark on the surface (pontilmark).

PORPHYRY A dense, very hard red volcanic stone, found at Djebel Dokhan (Mons Porphyrites) in Egypt. In ancient times it was often reserved for decoration in imperial families. Green porphyry is a very hard green granite from Laconia, sometimes wrongly called 'serpentine'.

PORTABLE / PORTATIVE ICON A form of icon; sometimes executed in mosaic, which became very popular in the Byzantine period, some examples dating from the 12th century. Thin tablets of wood of manageable size had tesserae fixed to them with gum mastic or a wax derivative adhesive. The resultant icons were often executed in the manner of miniatures and with great dexterity. They were probably derived from Classical portraiture, which in time took on theological significance. The icons were the forerunners of mosaics today, i.e. portable and for the most part on a wooden backing. **See *easel mosaic.***

PORTABLE MOSAIC (external) Make a simple frame from strips of wood, butt the ends or mitre the corners, and glue or nail together for rigidity. Grease the inner area of the frame with Vaseline or other releasing agent. Place over strong paper, and draw the inner outline of the frame on the paper. Remove the frame and begin to lay tesserae face down on the paper. On completion replace the frame, and cover the mosaic with a 2cm / 1in layer of a sand and cement mortar. Reinforce the mortar with wire, and add a further layer of mortar. Allow to cure slowly in a damp environment and after about four days ease the slab out of the frame (this can be re-used). Turn over, moisten the backing paper and peel it off. Grout the mosaic and clean any residue cement with a mortar cleaner. The finished piece can be used as an external pavement slab.

PORTASANTA A reddish marble veined with yellow, grey and white, from the Greek island of Chios (Khios).

PORTLAND CEMENT A staple in mosaic making, superb for many mosaic uses. It is a cement, white or grey in colour (simulating the colour of Portland stone in England). Always store cement in dry conditions and observe its shelf life – it should always feel silky. Its adhesive properties are greatly enhanced and strengthened by the addition of sand, or sand and lime or other plasticizers. It may, however, contain soluble salts that may look whitish on the surface, and if used in moist conditions they may increase porosity and cause deterioration.

PORTRAIT MOSAIC Some of the earliest portraits

in mosaic are thought to be of Alexander the Great, who can be seen in the 4th-century BC pebble pavement at Pella in his homeland of Macedonia, Greece. A further portrait of the great warrior may also be in the mosaic of Alexander and Darius III, King of Persia, in the so-called 'Battle of Issus' mosaic, before AD 79, which is believed to be derived from a painting and is now in the Archaeological Museum, Naples, Italy. Later, Byzantine heads of emperors, warriors and saints are masterly in their depiction, whether from reality or imagination, and the art of mosaic portraits continues to fascinate artists to this day.

Portrait mosaic
OEPINOΣ, OEPINOC, OEPINOY; Warrior saint, detail, 5th century AD, mosaic gold, smalti. (EMG)

The Rotunda of St George, Thessaloniki, Greece, built c.AD 306 was designed originally as a circular temple or a mausoleum. During the 5th century it was converted to a church and ornamented in the dome, the bays, lunettes and upper cylindrical walls, with sumptuous mosaics that are considered to be the earliest mural mosaics in the Middle East. The author was privileged to spend time studying the mosaics face on, on high scaffolding (erected to restore the mosaics after the damage caused by the 1978 earthquake). All the mosaic work is rich in texture and decoration, with a wealth of colour and imagery. A line of 15 martyrs, including warrior saints, bishops and courtiers, is outstanding for the portraiture. This military saint, with his accompanying inscription is a portrait of memorable quality, a true portrait encompassing character and humanity and yet resplendent with luminous spiritual detachment. It is a remarkable masterpiece by an enlightened Byzantine master artist.

POUNCE A chalk or fine powder.

POUNCING / PRICKING OUT A transfer method used to mark the outline, main lines or features of a mosaic. Punch through a cartoon following the main design features with a hole punch or tracing wheel, leaving a line of dots. The cartoon is then placed over the setting bed, or fixed to a wall, and the dots can be dusted or painted over on the cartoon, which is then removed to reveal a series of dots on the surface that is to take the mosaic. These can be joined up to complete the transfer. **See *transferring*.**

POZZOLANA A naturally occurring volcanic earth, found in Roman times in the vicinity of Pozzuoli in the Bay of Naples. It contains de-composable silicates, which, when ground and added to slaked lime, give a hydraulic plaster with good adhesive properties, thus making it more usable and forming a strong plaster of low porosity. Other materials with varying degrees of hydraulic properties include volcanic ash, powdered tile and brick and potsherds from clay, which have a high silica content. Further sources include earth from the volcanic islands of Santorini and Aspronisi.

PRECIOUS / SEMI-PRECIOUS STONES See **stones.**

PRIME A preparation of the surface of a backing board for working on; e.g. applying a PVA wash to a plywood base to aid adhesion.

Prime – wood preparation
Many modern mosaicists use plywood and other timber as a backing for their portable mosaic panels. All wood benefits from the application of a sealant to the surface to aid the adhesive properties of securing tesserae of glass, metal foils, and ceramic and marbles to its surface. A simple coating with a proprietary wood sealant on the exposed cut edge, as well as the top and bottom surfaces of the wood, will also help against moisture absorption and warping. This panel – a work by the author inspired by a visit to the sacred island of Delos in Greece – is benefiting from a further coating of dilute PVA before glass and marble tesserae complete the work. (JM)

PROTOME The forepart of an animal used in decorative design.

PUMICE STONE A vitreous volcanic rock that may be used as a light abrasive for work on the surface of a mosaic.

PUTTO (pl. **putti**) A chubby naked boy, a popular image found in many decorative Roman pavements, such as Piazza Armerina, Sicily, 4th century AD.

PVA (polyvinyl acetate adhesive) An indispensable watersoluble resin adhesive. PVA glue can be used diluted for a watersoluble adhesive in the indirect method of laying. It is a milk-white adhesive that becomes colourless when dry, with excellent bonding qualities on porous and textured materials. When dry it is water resistant but *not* waterproof. Some PVA glues become waterproof only when mixed with cement.

Prime
Walking on Light, 2003 by Elaine M Goodwin, 60cm x 60cm / 24in x 24in, mirror glass, platinum, white gold and marble. (J. Balfour-Paul collection.) (JM)

(See previous caption.) The sacred island of Delos in the Cyclades in the Aegean Sea is said to be the birthplace of Apollo, god of light. It holds some of the very earliest mosaics composed of coloured glass tesserae, onyx and agate. Mosaics were a status symbol for people in the Hellenistic world, and many of the intricate emblemata in the stately villas have characteristic black backgrounds and mosaics with highly detailed designs and minute tesserae in opus vermiculatum, e.g. Dionysus riding his Panther in the House of the Masks, c. 2nd century BC. The site of the uninhabited island, the sacred lake, the mythology surrounding it – and the mosaics – are a truly inspirational experience.

QUADRATUM See *opus quadratum.*

QUICKLIME Calcium oxide (CaO). A caustic, porous, whitish substance used in mosaic mortars.

RAINBOW CABLE A pattern made up of multicoloured bands of tesserae.

RAINBOW STYLE An ornamental style in which lines of tesserae, each in a single colour, are set diagonally on edge; i.e. a style of mosaic in which the colours of the tesserae are arranged in a diagonal sequence rather than in rows. A superb example is the rainbow 'glory' in the dome of the Rotunda of St George, Thessaloniki, Greece, late 4th–6th century.

REALISM (naturalism) A style that aspires to achieve a physical likeness to something, as in a figure or face, thus becoming as much like the 'natural' as possible.

Rainbow style
Rainbow Sampler – vitreous glass on wood.

This sampler demonstrates the capability of mosaic to take on a rich textural effect by the simplest of means. A repeated placing of a set of rainbow-simulating colours set on the diagonal can create a dazzling pattern, as each colour 'bleeds' into the adjacent colour. Rainbow cable designs intrigued the ancient mosaicist: examples appear throughout the Greco–Roman and Byzantine eras, on border designs for floors and as rich decorative bands in cupolas.

REBATE In a mosaic the distance a pebble or tessera protrudes above a finished surface, i.e. where the mortar surface is somewhat lower.

REBATE / RABBET A continuous rectangular groove or step cut on an edge, as on a frame surrounding a mosaic.

RECEDING COLOURS Cool or pale colours, often blue or green or violet, that seem to retreat or move back in an artwork.

RECIPROCAL See *double reverse method.*

REDUCING GLASS A concave glass, used for viewing the work as a whole. This is mainly used in large-scale projects for an overview. When looked through, the design appears smaller and more compact, therefore it is an aid to gauge balance, proportion in area, colour and texture.

REGISTRATION MARKS Marks that indicate alignment or joins, made to help keep the angle and placing of the tesserae continuous and true. They are used as an aid when drawing repeated patterns, as in borders, and also when joining together separately made panels to form a whole. They are often employed on the paper backing of large-scale works using the indirect method of mosaic making – though not exclusively.

REINFORCED CONCRETE A durable concrete that is both weather- and water-proof. It has expanded metal, metal mesh, reinforcing mesh or steel or iron rods embedded between layers of cement mortar. The term also applies to an armature or a support for 2D and 3D mosaics that uses a metal frame under the mortar.

RELEASE AGENT This may be Vaseline, petroleum jelly, or even margarine! It is used to grease wooden frames, etc., used in making up concrete panels or slabs. It allows for the easy release of the panel. **See** *parting agent.*

RELIEF MOSAIC A mosaic panel that has high or low relief work. This may arise from materials being set on edge to project above the surface, or cut away from the surface. In all cases the varying heights of the tesserae exert a play of shadow over the surface and increase the textural and lively qualities.

RELIEF TILES Tiles that have a raised design and can be used to add texture to mural work.

REPERTORY A collection of patterns, motifs and designs by mosaicists of all eras. **See** *pattern books; copy books.*

REPLICA An exact, or nearly so, copy or version of another. A replica of a mosaic may be made by pressing wet papier mâché on to the surface, thus recording each tessera and its height and angle (and colour), and then producing from this negative mould a cast copy to record each tessera; tedious but true. **See** *laying: reverse method, indirect method.*

REPOUSSÉ A relief produced by hammering metal from the back.

RESIN Used as an adhesive with glass fibre for obtaining a lightweight backing support. It is also used for reinforcement. Clear resin is also used by specialist contractors to bind aggregates of marble and glass chippings to provide a hard-wearing surface, which could be incorporated into mosaic work or surround mosaic panels in pathways, pools or flooring. **See** *fibreglass; epoxy resins.*

RESTORATION AND RECONSTRUCTION Techniques to preserve and repair crumbling (ancient) mosaics. Previously liquid cement was injected into the back of mosaic works but this became outdated, mainly due to the heaviness of the concrete panels produced. Nowadays epoxy resins and vermiculite granules are used in layers for lightness and strength, and fixing bolts are inserted at the same time for easy placement.

RETICULATUM See *opus reticulatum.*

REVERSE OR PARCEL MOSAIC See *indirect method.*

Relief mosaic
For and Against, detail, 1978 by Jane Muir, Open University, Milton Keynes, England;
1.20m x 3m / 48in x 118in, marble, slate, smalti, limestone.

The artist Jane Muir (b. 1929) was born in London and trained at both
Middlesbrough and Teesside Colleges of Art. She studied mosaic techniques in Italy
from the 1950s, becoming a founder member of the International Association of
Contemporary Mosaic (AIMC) in Ravenna, Italy, in 1975. She experimented with
innovative mosaic techniques in the 1970s, incorporating glass fusions and found
objects into her work. She continues to explore the medium alongside drawing,
etching and most recently watercolour painting, inspired by early music. This early
photograph shows the artist, ever intrigued by processes, at work on a vertically
produced relief mosaic incorporating shards of riven Welsh slate set on edge to
introduce a directional dynamic in contrast to the softer, larger Delabole slate
tesserae that make up a more uniform background.

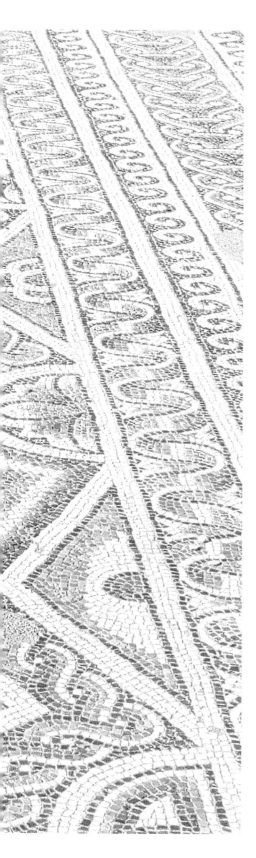

RHOMBUS (Greek: *rhombos*) An equilateral parallelogram or diamond shape, often employed in a variety of designs in ancient mosaics.

RINCEAU An ornamental motif of sinuous branching scrolls made of plant stems and leaves, and elaborated with other natural forms.

RIVEN MARBLE Marble cut to expose the crystalline, more textural surface.

RIVER An area where lines of grouting have inadvertently come together because of a build-up of successive lines of tesserae to form a seeming 'crack'; a thing to be aware of and avoided since it acts as a visually disturbing line that attracts the eye in an unpleasing manner.

ROCKS Aggregates of various materials formed from volcanic, sedimentary and metamorphic sources. They are used for beddings and foundations.

ROD A monochrome segment of glass cut from a trail or drawn strand, as used in micro mosaics. **See filato.**

ROLLING PIN A useful tool (really!) for pressing mosaic evenly down into cement, especially useful employed over or around curved surfaces.

Rhombus
Early Christian Basilica, 6th century, detail,
Amphipolis, North Greece. (EMG)

Amphipolis was a prosperous city in Classical Greek, Hellenistic and Roman times, with the famous road, the Via Egnatia, passing through it. St Paul is said to have passed that way in AD 49/50, and the spread of Christianity was encouraged. There are four early Christian basilicas, resplendent with polychrome mosaics. Some of the floors depict transitional pagan/Christian imagery: peacocks, drinking stags, and a plethora of birds and fish. This nave floor (Basilica G) is distinguished by its sophisticated geometry. The central design is a fire-wheel set in a square surrounded by intersecting geometric braids, rhomboids, octagons, hexagons, rosettes and stars – a wonderful array, set in a frame of bands of ivy leaves, braid guilloche and wave crests. Beautiful, restrained in colour and complete!

Running pliers – demonstration
These are glass-cutting pliers, characterized by a notch in the centre of the
bottom jaw, which are used for snapping straight edges. After scoring a straight
line with the glass cutter (which is often part of the cutter too), align the centre
of the cutter with the score line, letting the 'wings' of the cutter rest evenly under
the glass, and squeeze the handles of the cutter together. A crack runs along the
score line and the glass is cleanly cut. (JM)

ROMAN MOSAICS Glass tesserae and mosaics of both the ancient Roman world and of the Vatican workshop in Rome, Italy.

ROSETTE A decorative motif in the form of a flower with radiating petals that is used in many a Roman pavement.

ROSSO ANTICO A red marble from Taenarum, in the southern Peloponnese.

ROTINO (It. 'little wheel') A very small manually operated grinding wheel, running on a free axle.

'ROUGHENING' The abrading of the surface of mortar for better articulation, particularly between coats of mortar when preparing a setting bed for floor or wall.

ROUNDEL / RONDEL A circular disc; in particular a unique mouth-blown and hand spun disc of glass, incorporating imperfections and bubbles, etc. They are popularly used in decorative mosaics.

RUDUS (L. 'rubble') In classical pavement-making, referring to the lowest layer of mortar in the foundation bed of a mosaic floor.

RUNNING LINE A length of tesserae of narrow oblong shape that is used to delineate or outline a motif or figure.

RUNNING PLIERS (also running cutters, breaking pliers) Tools used to cut glass after scoring. Apply an even pressure either side of the score line by gently squeezing the legs of the pliers together.

RUSTICO MOSAIC (Fr. *rocaille*) A wall or floor made up of a melange of pebbles, shells, limestone, or glass, as seen in grottoes, gardens and fountains in the 16th, 17th and 18th centuries, originating from classical Roman nymphaea decoration that utilized shells, pumice, marble and glass.

SAFETY Wear protective clothing; goggles or eye shields for flying splinters, and a facemask, dust respirator or air filtering mask for dust-filled air or vapours. When using nippers, cut away from the face and to the side. Be sure to wear latex, rubber or plastic gloves when working with cements and acid cleaning. Read all packaging carefully and observe all the precautions. In the work area maintain good ventilation. Clean the working area from time to time and try to keep it clutter-free, and be constantly aware of any potential dangers. **See *eye shields.***

SALVAGED MATERIALS These are useful free additions to traditional mosaic materials, and include sea-washed glass and pottery, driftwood, coins, old metals, etc.

SAMIAN WARE A generic term for the fine red-gloss pottery from Gaul, Germany and the Mediterranean, made between the 1st and 3rd centuries AD. It was often used as a useful source for red colour in Roman mosaics, being a finer material than broken tile. Its use has enabled mosaics to be dated. It is also known as *terra sigillata.*

SAND A form of silica used in glassmaking. A very important element is the quality of the sand used in making mosaic smalti; it should be very fine for ease of fusion, washed, dried and sieved. Sand is composed of a mass of tiny fragments and particles of stone and other minerals, containing siliceous, micaceous, calcareous and even precious minerals. There are various types of sands, e.g. sharp sand, which has large particles, and soft sand, which is fine and used for making mortars. There are also a great variety of colours, e.g. silver, red, yellow, grey, etc. Sand can also be used, plus an adhesive, on its own for grouting.

SANDERS Tools used to smooth the edges of tesserae and sometimes used to improve the shape of circular shapes after cutting. They should be obtainable as diamond-coated, small pads with a foam base. Use wet or dry.

SARCOPHAGUS A container or tomb that contained a dead body. It is generally constructed of marble or stone and occasionally decorated with mosaic; for example, late 4th century sarcophagi with mosaic figures of the deceased can be seen in the Bardo Museum, Tunisia.

SATURATED COLOUR Colour at its most intense.

SAW There are a great many saws used from time to time in mosaic making. Bow saws, wet/dry saws, or diamond band-saws are useful tools for cutting or slicing stone, having a narrow blade that can be operated manually or electrically. An oscillating saw can sometimes be whetted with sand or emery and water to cut glass, ceramic, porcelain, lead, copper, zinc and plastic, etc. Hacksaws are good for cutting handmade fibre resin sheets, and hand or electric saws for timber cutting.

SCALE An accidental inclusion in glass, formed from a corrosive product from the metal implements used during its making. As with all imperfections in glass, mosaicists often use these to advantage.

SCALE DRAWINGS It is useful to show these to clients for prospective commissions or projects, e.g. 1:50 would amount to 1cm (^{3}/8in) on the plan or sketch to 50cm (20in) in reality. Useful scales are as follows: 1:10 on projects up to 5m (16 ft); 1:20 for projects over 5m (16 ft); 1:5 for small projects up to 2m (6 ft) in size.

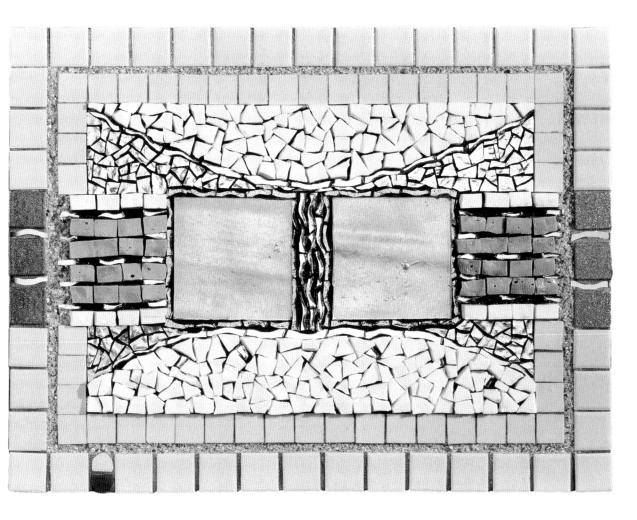

Sand

Serenissima IV, 2003, Elaine M Goodwin, 40cm x 30cm / 16in x 12in, smalti, white gold, ceramic, platinum, mirror glass, silver sand. (Private collection.) (JM)

The author, the artist Elaine M Goodwin, is a frequent traveller, ever in search of mosaics from the ancient or modern world. On and around sites she collects stones, pebbles, marbles and sands that are used in subsequent works – sometimes as *aide-mémoires* to give direct links to a particular place and experience, or used purely for textural and aesthetic interest. In this work, one of a series evoking thoughts on her beloved Venice, the artist uses a sharp silver sand containing reflective particles of mica, as part of the framing panel to continue the light, elusive theme of the work.

Scales – opus panel
Scale design, 1999 by Elaine M Goodwin and Group 5, wall panel, Royal Albert Memorial Museum and Art Gallery, Exeter, England, 50cm x 152cm / 20in x 60in, ceramic, glass, mirror. (JM)

In 1999 the Royal Albert Memorial Museum and Art Gallery commissioned the author, Elaine M Goodwin, to design a mosaic vestibule adjoining two main galleries, in conjunction with the Millennium exhibition *Mosaic: A Living Art 2001*. This panel and others were made as demonstration panels by the artist and three members of her Group 5 – Glen Morgan, Eve Jennings and Rhonwen Vickers. This vertical wall panel of scale shapes demonstrates one of the variations of the scallop shape design, a frequent motif in ancient mosaic work, and seen today in modern pavings and walkways. Sometimes the outlines of the shape are emphasized, at other times the central vortex is highlighted.

SCALES A popular geometric shape with scallop-like formation seen in many borders in Roman mosaics and also in background designs, e.g. the Imperial Palace mosaics, 4th century, Istanbul, Turkey. It is used today as an apt ground for marine- and water-themed mosaics. Also known as scallop or shell design.

SCALPEL A sharp cutting knife, useful to a mosaicist in so many ways, including the removal of excess areas of cement from mosaic edges after the cement has hardened, and for scoring a wooden backing panel before commencing work, and so on. **See *score.***

SCISSORS There are various sizes and shapes, used to cut backing paper, netting, plastic sheeting, etc.

SCORE To lightly mark or graze the glass when using a scoring tool or glass cutter before snapping or breaking. Score lines are also made to 'rough up' wood or cement by using a knife or trowel to form an invaluable key before fixing the mosaic pieces.

SCRATCH COAT The first plaster coat applied to a wall, when preparing it for working *in situ.*

SCREWDRIVER An indispensable tool for lifting misplaced pieces!

SCRIM A coarse heavy cloth, useful for cleaning the mosaic surface after grouting and utilized also in the building up of a form on an armature. Soak the cloth in water first, to wet it thoroughly, squeeze dry and then immerse it in a cement slurry, lift and apply to the armature. **See *armature; hessian.***

SCULPTURAL MOSAICS Many present-day mosaicists are working on three-dimensional or sculptural works, both as freestanding sculptures and in the area of design as furniture. Mosaic is sometimes applied also as a decorative or textural skin to a preformed shape, or more interestingly, as an integral part of a sculptural work. *(Illustrated on following page.)* **See *armature.***

SCUTULATUM See *opus scutulatum.*

SEALERS (stain stops) Generally proprietary liquids, often of silicon, which provide a necessary application for some marble, ceramic and porcelain finishes. Always seal a mosaic surface when it is completely dry, as moisture can be trapped within and a milky film could discolour the surface under the sealant. It is sometimes also advisable to seal tesserae before grouting in order to stop any added grouting colour seeping into porous tiles. **See *impregnator.***

SECONDARY COLOURS In the colour cycle, green, violet and orange are the three colours made by mixing the three pairs of complementary primary colours: red and yellow to make orange; blue and yellow to make green; and blue and red to make violet. These are simple facts to know about when juxtaposing colours in a mosaic design that is to be viewed at some distance. **See *juxtaposition; optical mixing.***

SECTILE From Latin *secare*, 'to cut'. **See *opus sectile.***

SEED Minute bubbles found in glass, which may add interest when used in making up a mosaic.

SEMIS A decorative system or a pattern made up of small decorative elements (*sémi*) scattered at random or at regular intervals in a white field, without a formal framework. They are used to create simple floral and decorative elements in a pavement, e.g. 'diamonds' or small crosses.

SET SQUARE A useful tool for squaring off edges, that can also be used as a straight edge or ruler.

SETTING BED The final thin layer of mortar into which the tesserae are set. **See *giornata.***

SETTING MOSAICS There are three different methods. (1) **Direct**: where the tesserae are placed individually on to a base or into a bedding mortar. (2) **Double reverse** or reciprocal: where the tesserae are bedded face up in sand or plasticine, and paper or cloth is temporarily glued to the upper surface. When the glue is dry, the mosaic is lifted and placed in a permanent bedding mortar, and after the mortar has set the temporary facing material is soaked and removed and the whole mosaic grouted on site. (3) **Indirect/reverse**: where the tesserae are glued temporarily face down on to a (coloured)

Sculptural mosaics

A l'Aube du Troisième Millénaire, front view & back view, 1999 by Verdiano Marzi, Collège Villars, Denain (France du Nord), France, smalti, black Irish marble, Brittany granite.

The Italian artist Verdiano Marzi (b. 1949) was born in Ravenna, Italy, where he studied at the Academy of Fine Art before moving to Paris in 1973 to study at l'Ecole des Beaux Arts. He now lives and works in France. The artist frequently works on monumental sculptural mosaics, sensitively attuned to the siting of each work. His work is characterized by strong colour combinations between areas of intricately cut tesserae and broad areas of stone, glass or marble. This millennium sculpture, for a new college, was designed as an open book consisting of three parts: two side panels worked directly on to black marble, and a free-standing spine of yellow granite. The first thousand years are represented by the moon, water and ancient hieroglyphics on the left-hand side, which create a dialogue with the sun, fire and scripts on the right-hand side, symbolic of the second millennium. These combine to give rise to the new third millennium, in a stele-shaped central panel devoid of mosaic – the century was as then unsung.

cartoon or thick paper or cloth, and the mosaic constructed in reverse. The work is then lifted, turned over, and fixed into a permanent site, and the backing paper, cartoon or cloth washed off. Again the mosaic is grouted and cleaned on site. For more information **see** *direct method*; *indirect method*; **and** *laying*.

SETTING TESSERAE A variety of possibilities exist to enhance a mosaic surface. Using the direct method the tesserae may be applied at an angle, tilted sideways or upwards/downwards towards the light. Great variation may also be made in the width of the interstices. Alternatively tesserae may be used of any thickness or any shape, and set on edge to add a variety of heights and textures. **See** *angle of tesserae; relief mosaic.*

SETTS Riven paving blocks that may be made of stone or granite.

SGRAFFITO (pl. **sgraffiti**) Scratched-away areas of the surface of a work of art.

SHALE A clay schist, generally with a fine grain.

SHEETING Polythene or plastic, especially of a horticultural grade, is used as a waterproof membrane when preparing ground for external mosaics. It is also used, cut to size and placed between the drawing and netting, in the direct method of laying mosaic to stop the adhesive used in the mosaic making from sticking to the drawing but allowing the drawing to be seen.

SHELLAC A thin varnish made from vegetable resin and denatured alcohol. It is now rarely used on the surface of finished mosaics because of flaking and discoloration.

SHELLS A natural and found material used since Roman times. For example, in front of the Casa delle Colonne Mosaici at Pompeii, Italy (before AD 79) four mosaic columns were found that were supporting a covered pavilion and whose Doric capitals were outlined in shells (Museo Archeologico, Naples, Italy). When using shells, sort them by colour, size and shape. Of especial interest to mosaicists are the nacreous qualities of abalone and mother of pearl.

Setting tesserae
Golden Panel, 2002 by Elaine M Goodwin, 30cm x 30cm / 12in x 12in, Venetian gold leaf, ceramic. (JM)

The very early Byzantine mosaic masters of the 6th to 8th centuries AD understood light. They knew that by angling their materials of gold and smalti towards or away from the available light source, they could create surfaces on which light could play to create an ambience of wonderment and spiritual power when contemplated by a supplicant, whether Muslim or Christian. This small panel was made by Elaine M Goodwin to reveal how some aspects of light can be manipulated by the artist in the placing of the tesserae, in a sequence of angles, either to give a sense of movement or to evoke a surface ambiguity by trying to dematerialize the backing support, as the Byzantine mosaicists were able to do within the architectural planes of mosque and basilica.

SICKLE STONE A file made of carborundum, used to smooth sharp edges.

SIGNINUM A crushed tile and lime mortar that is both strong and damp resistant. The smooth pink-coloured cement mortar is of great strength and has good waterproof qualities when containing an aggregate made of crushed terracotta. It is called after the Italian town of Segni (Roman name Signia), from which the material is said to have originated. **See *opus signinum*.**

SILHOUETTE MOSAIC A figurative mosaic in black and white. In Classical times it was a popular fashion, e.g. in Ostia, 1st–3rd century AD. Such mosaics were usually made of black tesserae on a white ground, with some delineation in white on the black figures.

SILICONE (any derivative of the non-metallic element silicon) Used for an edging infill to seal any gaps after fixing mosaics to an interior surface. It is often available in cartridges for use in a mastic gun, and it dries thick but slightly rubbery, allowing for flexibility of movement (i.e. contraction and expansion), and is water-resistant. Use it on dry, clean surfaces. Silicone liquid is used on marble mosaics for waterproofing and to prevent the staining of porous surfaces during the grouting process. Shake the container and pour a few drops on a cloth and polish vigorously. Let it soak into the surface for about 30 minutes, and wipe and polish again. Clear silicone is available from specialist glaziers. **See *sealers*.**

SILICONE PAPER A paper coated with silicone and having anti-adhesive properties. It is used in fibre netting techniques of mosaic making in lieu of plastic sheeting.

SILVER METAL This has a beautiful lustre but is less resistant to corrosion than gold. **See *gold*.**

SINOPIA A red ochre from Cappadocia, Turkey, used for painting and exported from Sinope (now Sinop) on the Black Sea. It is also used for preliminary drawing directly on to the ground or cement mortar to provide the basic guide lines in the making of a mosaic. These drawn lines or *sinopie* (pl.) may be seen, for example, in the dome of the 6th-century Rotonda of Hagios Georgios in Thessaloniki, Greece.

SINTERED MOSAIC Vitreous glass mosaic ground and heated to an extremely high temperature and pressed. It is very durable, non-absorbent, tough and resistant to extremes of temperature, and is therefore used frequently for commercial mosaics and in public thoroughfares.

SKETCH A preliminary or preparatory drawing that usually begins with a few rough, visual concepts or outlines made on paper, or directly on to a wooden base, or even as an under-painting on a wall. These initial sketched marks should be suggestive and freely rendered, and allowed to develop naturally.

SLAKED LIME A quicklime with added water. It can be used as a fine, soft powder (hydrated lime) or as a plastic-like substance (lime putty).

Silhouette mosaic
Athlete (detail), 1937, from the Foro Italico, Viale dell'Impero, Rome, Italy: black and white marble. (EMG)

The Foro Italico (formerly known as Foro Mussolini) is an extraordinary testimony to early 20th-century politics in art and architecture. A modern Italian Imperial statement, it incorporates a sports stadium that has a floor of over 1,500 square metres / approx. 2,000 square yards of mosaic work, carried out by the mosaic school at Spilimbergo in the Friuli region of north-east Italy. Many well-known artists such as Gino Severini, Giulio Rosso, Angelo Canevari and Achille Capizzano were involved in designing the mosaics. They chose to work in the silhouette style, using black and white marble, inspired by the 1st–3rd century AD mosaics of the nearby port of Ostia. The designs show athletes and gymnasts alongside historical depictions of Rome's great and mythological past. All is depicted in a restrained yet powerfully monumental style, as befits an Olympic stadium.

SLATE A hard, waterproof rock made of layers of shale and clay that can be carved, pressed, riven, knapped, or set on end, etc. It has a natural matt finish, and is divisible into sheets for use in mosaic. Use a broad-edge chisel and a lump hammer to cut the slate in slices, or split it with a hammer and bolster before using a diamond blade saw to cut into shape; then dress it, that is, shape it with a slate knife over a hard metal edge. Mosaic nippers can also be used to cut the edges to a required shape.

SLIP A clay with water added to form a smooth and runny liquid.

SLIP-RESISTANT FINISH A quality inherent in many tiles used in mosaic making, e.g. vitreous glass, as used in swimming pools. To aid the non-slip quality of a mosaic surface it may be necessary to make larger interstices, which will in turn introduce large areas of slip-proof grout.

SLURRY A mixture of cement, sand and lime plaster, mixed with extra water. It is brushed on to a wetted cement wall or pavement before applying the next coat of mortar, to help adhesion. It is also used for soaking scrim or gauze when building up a 3D mosaic form on an armature.

SMALTI FILATI (spun smalti) A dense glass of many and various colours, drawn into thin strings or threads and cut into slices for use in miniature mosaics. It was invented and developed in the Vatican workshops of Rome during the second part of the 18th century.

Slate
Ancestors – Foundation, 1999 by Dugald MacInnes (frame: Duncan Donaldson), 64cm x 64cm / 25in x 25in, slate, smalti, Venetian gold leaf.

The Scottish artist Dugald MacInnes was born in Argyll and studied mosaic mural art under the mosaicist George Garson at the Glasgow School of Art (1970–75). He later gained qualifications in Geology and Field Archaeology, interests which motivate his art work. An intense relationship with the land of Scotland, its ancient formation and prehistoric mystery, colours and inspires the artist's work. The artist uses slate from discarded quarries in all his work; its age – over 500 million years – and its quality – soft and dark – never fails to evoke continual enquiry. Traditional materials such as Venetian smalti and gold play their role in the work, introducing colour and focal points of light into a darkly brooding palette.

SMALTO (pl. **smalti**) Generally referred to in the plural, this is the most coveted of mosaic glass. It is today made primarily in Venice, though Mexico and Russia also produce glass smalti. It is usually an opaque and brilliant glass with a high lead content. The secrets of the hand-coloured, hand-cut material are passed down through generations, the most notable and best-known workshop being the Angelo Orsoni syndicate in Cannaregio, Venice. Thousands of colours are available and it can be obtained in 'pizza' (disc or 'plate') form or cut to size. Smalti is also known as Venetian glass, Byzantine glass, Venetian 'enamel', glass mosaic, artistic glass, and is sometimes wrongly termed 'enamel'.

Smalti is a vitreous paste or handmade glass, made up of a mix of silica and alkaline substances like potash, lead or soda-lime. A great variety of metal oxides have been added to this basic mix, throughout the long history of smalti making, to act as colouring agents: e.g. blue is obtained from cobalt oxide; blue-green from cobalt oxide and added cupric oxide; ruby red from selenium dioxide and cadmium sulphide; purple from manganese dioxide and tellurium oxide; pink from selenium oxide and antimoniate of lead; yellow from cerium dioxide, titanium dioxide, iron oxide and uranium oxide; and green from copper oxide, copper carbonate and chromium oxide. The mix is melted at controlled temperatures, varying with each colour. The viscous mixture is poured into a flat metal disc, round or oblong, and allowed to cool or anneal at controlled rates. The resulting 'pancake' or 'pizza' is then scored and hand cut into fairly regular rectangular pieces or cubes (around 13 x 10 x 10mm / $^1/_2$ x $^3/_8$ x $^3/_8$ in). The fractured edge reveals the brilliant colour of the often uneven surface of the glass. This is the side generally exposed in setting a mosaic. The rich colour and reflective sparkle of smalti is unrivalled in mosaic. The colour range continues to be extensive, as colours can be custom-made to order, and the material is relatively expensive to purchase. The tesserae are completely lightproof and weatherproof and have an incomparable brilliance and the choice of colours is infinite. **See *annealing.***

SMALTO ANTICO / SMALTI ANTICI (antique smalti) In order to reproduce ancient Byzantine glass, which has a less reflective quality than modern smalti, sand is added in greater quantities at the

Smalti

Where Will You be in the Year 3000?, 2000 by Mireille Lévesque, 60cm x 60cm / 24in x 24in, mixed media, smalti, porcelain, Quebec slate.

The Canadian artist Mireille Lévesque was born in Quebec and studied Fine Art at the University of Quebec in Montreal in 1990. She worked as a painter and silkscreen artist and evolved a series of work in which repetition was to the fore. During the 1990s she studied stone cutting and mosaic in both Italy and England before deciding to devote her energies to mosaic, a timeless medium. Inspired by nature, around the St Lawrence River where she lives, the artist incorporates local stones, shales and rocks alongside the more traditional smalti into her work, often with a disarming *naïveté*.

melting stage of the process to produce a grainier, more textured, less light-reflecting glass.

SNAPLINE This is used in mural making to mark straight lines. A length of powder-coated or chalk-dust-impregnated string is fixed or held taut at the two ends. By pulling back the string from the centre of its length and releasing it against the wall a straight line is created. Great when working on site on large wall murals.

SOLDERING IRON An excellent tool for joining metals; they can be electric or gas powered. They are especially useful in building and constructing iron and metal armatures for base structures as reinforcement for 3D mosaics.

SOREL CEMENT See *magnesite*.

SPANDREL The triangular shape between two curves and between the springing and centre of an arch. On a pavement it denotes the area between the corners of a square and an inscribed circle.

SPATULA A tool with a flexible, flat end, that can be of plastic or wood. It is used for applying adhesive to tesserae, and for any mixing or spreading work.

SPIZZI (It.) Mosaic tiles that are regularly small, of 10 x 10mm / $^3/_8$ x $^3/_8$ in.

SPIZZIONI (It.) The most common size of bought tesserae, of 20 x 20mm / $^3/_4$ x $^3/_4$ in.

SPOLVERO (It. *spolverare*) The small dust dots used as a reference for the mosaicist. **See *pouncing*.**

SPONGE A builder's sponge is an indispensable object. It is a very absorbent sponge used for moistening the backing paper in the indirect method and also for cleaning off excessive cement from the surface of a mosaic.

SPREADER This can be notched, toothed or smooth-edged, and made of plastic or wood with a rubber blade. It is used for spreading grout or cement across the surface of a mosaic, or for applying cement over a base support.

SQUEEGEE A plastic or rubber blade used for scraping away excess grout or adhesive from the mosaic surface. **See *spreader; spatula*.**

STACCO (It. *staccare*, to detach / separate) The term is used in restoration when referring to the technique of removing a mosaic from a wall or floor.

STAINED GLASS This glass is also used in mosaic making and cut according to the shape needed. Various shapes and finishes are available, including antique glass, water glass, streaky, opalescent, iridescent, rolled glass, drawn glass, flashed glass, decorative glass and clear glass. It is frequently used in mosaic, backed with foils or 'leaf' to create brilliant light and colour effects. **See *window glass*.**

STATUMEN (L. *supporis*) Used by Vitruvius to refer to the layer of rubble underneath the mortar bedding of a mosaic pavement. It is the lowest bedding area of a mosaic foundation, and made up of fist-sized stones.

STEATITE A type of stone, usually green in colour.

STONE INTARSIA A form of decorative mosaic-like inlay, made from stones of a variety of colours, polished to a uniform and smooth surface.

STONES A general term for all the rocks and minerals used in mosaic making. Stones are very dense, hard, and may include many varieties. They are mostly composed of silicates, which are not susceptible to hydrochloric acid, or are calcareous, which are susceptible to acids, e.g. marbles and limestone. **See *Mohs scale, pietre dure*.**

STONES (semi-precious and precious) These have been used since antiquity in mosaic work and add areas of rich colour or opulence. They may include **agate**: a hard, fine-grained stone, which is often banded in concentric circles or rings and may vary from blue to rich orange; **alabaster**: a fine-grained, translucent gypsum, which is found in white to reddish-brown; **amethyst**: a semiprecious quartz, which is lavender to purple in colour; **carnelian/cornelian**: a hard chalcedony of a bright and lively red; **chalcedony**: a translucent to transparent quartz, which may be white, grey, blue or brown; **jade**: a silicate which is white or of various shades of green; **jasper**: which is often speckled,

banded or striated, and found in shades of red, yellow, green and grey-blue; **lapis lazuli**: a limestone of deep blue, violet, or greenish-blue, often flecked with iron pyrites; **malachite**: a mineral and gem, translucent or opaque, and greenish in colour; **obsidian**: a volcanic glass obtained from lava, which can be black, red, brown or a greenish colour; **onyx**: a fine-grained agate usually of contrasting colours, deep red or brown-red – Tiger's eye, cat's eye, and falcon's eye are all

Stones

Offering, 2003 by Elaine M Goodwin, lapis lazuli, iron pyrites, Venetian gold, ceramic. (Collection G. Webb.) (JM)

A small centrally placed lapis lazuli stone, collected when the author travelled in Afghanistan in the 1980s, is celebrated in this tiny mosaic icon – an homage. Iron pyrites, a mineral compound often found embedded in lapis lazuli, is a material much used by the artist as an integral part of the work. Known colloquially as 'fool's gold', it acts as a visual and symbolic counterpoint to any truly precious gold used.

Studio

The English artist Elaine M Goodwin in her studio in Exeter, UK. The artist has been working in the mosaic medium since leaving Exeter College of Art and Design where she studied sculpture. The shelves are arranged with jars of Venetian smalti, some of which belonged to Hans Unger and his pupil Hildegart Nicholas. The shelves also contain marbles from around the world, and gold from Orsoni's in Venice. Each tessera and each slab (*quadrato*) of gold awaits use. An artist's studio is such a personal space, and hours of work and contemplation make it the fulcrum of creative existence – a sanctum to the muse. (JM)

forms of onyx; **porphyry**: an igneous or volcanic rock, which is found in colours from reddish-purple to green; **topaz**: an aluminium silicate, which may be colourless, pale yellow or deep yellow; and **quartz**, which may be a variety of colours, translucency and opacity and ranges from a white/milky colour to brown, yellow and violet.

STONEWARE TILES These are made from a siliceous clay or clay and flint and are very highly fired. They are impervious to water and are therefore excellent for external use.

STREET MURALS These are public displays or works of mosaic art, often of decorative, political or environmental content. **See *mosaic mural.***

STUCCO This is a fine lime plaster used for decorative surfacing and relief work. Used as a binder, it sets slowly to a hard, durable surface.

STUCCO DECORATION An art form that evolved during the 1st century BC in Italy.

STUDIO An established place or workshop for making art.

STYLIZATION An interpretation of a motif that simplifies, exaggerates or emphasizes without ever completely losing understanding, and is used a great deal in mosaic work.

SUPPORT This is a foundation or backing panel for a mosaic; a solid and rigid base. **See *base.***

SUTURE This refers to a seam between two sections of mosaic, which may be executed at different times or by different craftsmen.

SWASTIKA An ancient Sanskrit word; a widely used motif, possibly representing the divinity of the sun and the sky, and symbolic of good fortune. It is used frequently in geometric mosaics and for border designs.

SYMBOLISM A motif, colour, pattern or sign, representational of something other than itself, and therefore understood by association.

TABLINUM A central room at the far end of an atrium in a Roman villa.

TABLION (pl. **tablia**) Large rectangular embroidery 'patches' let into the cloaks of some Byzantine processional mosaic figures, e.g. in the 'Procession of Emperor Justinian' in San Vitale, 6th century, Ravenna, Italy. **See *gammadion.***

TABULA PICTA An easel painting or mosaic.

TANIT (Punic goddess; sign of) Her religio–magical symbol, used in Phoenician and Punic cultures, is seen on Hellenistic mosaics in the Mediterranean, e.g. House of the Dolphins, Delos, Greece.

TARSIA An inlay. Tiny tesserae are cut according to a pattern and attached to a backing material that is integral and visible, unlike mosaic where the backing support is covered.

TEMPERA A liquid binding medium for a powdered pigment.

TEMPLATE A guide, made of card, metal or wood, etc., of the kind that has been used since Classical times to aid drawing. It is of particular use in geometric designs for mosaic making where repetition is called for.

TEPIDARIUM A moderately heated room in a Roman bath house, forming a transition area between the calidarium and frigidarium.

TERRACOTTA (lit. baked earth) The term usually means unglazed ceramic and sculpture. The colours range from orange to red to brown, depending on the composition of the earth. It also means baked clay, which is the material of tiles, pottery and bricks. The term can also refer again to colour. In the USA the term can even include glazed ware. If using terracotta as a base for mosaic, prime it first before laying an adhesive or cement as it is very porous and will absorb moisture thirstily.

TERRAZZO A modern Italian term for various forms of mortar and cement pavings, containing an aggregate. The random pieces of aggregate, which may be marble or stone chippings, can be used within a plain or coloured cement, before being ground smooth and polished. Terrazzo is also known as *pavimento veneziana.*

TERRAZZO TILES Tiles formed under hydraulic pressure into predetermined shapes and sizes.

TERTIARY COLOURS Of which there are six; blue/green, blue/violet, red/orange, red/violet, yellow/orange, yellow/green. They are made by mixing a primary colour with an adjacent secondary colour (each enhances the other).

TESSELLAE Diminutive of tesserae (Latin terminology). **See *abaculus.***

TESSELLARIUS / TESSERARIUS A person who specialized in opus tessellatum, i.e. in making floor mosaics.

TESSELLATE To make up a mosaic of units (i.e. tesserae).

TESSELLATUM See *opus tessellatum*.

Texture
Moroccan carpet (detail), Ethnography Museum, Essaouira, Morocco.

It is supposed by many mosaic historians that mosaic floors evolved from carpet making. There is a mosaic portrait in the Alexandria Archaeological Museum, Egypt, of Queen Berenice II, signed by the pictor imaginarius, Sophilos, 3rd century BC, which has mosaic 'fringes' composed of lead strips and tesserae. This carpet in the Ethnography Museum in Essaouira, on the western coast of Morocco, is rich in pattern and may well, in turn, have been influenced by the work of mosaicists.

TESSERA (pl. **tesserae**) A Latin term for any square object, which came originally from the Greek meaning 'four', implying a cube of stone, glass or terracotta. This is the most commonly used term today for the materials used in making a mosaic. They are the individual units, which can be of any size or shape, that make up a tessellated art work or mosaic. **See *abaculus*.**

TEXTURE The surface quality of a mosaic that results from the materials used, e.g. glass, stone, ceramic, and their inherent qualities of size, shape and surface finish. It may also include the andamento and the interstices.

Texture
Mosaic from Lixus (detail), Archaeological Museum, Tetouan, Morocco, 2nd–3rd century AD.

Roman mosaicists excelled at geometric designs in countless floors and border designs in countries all around the Mediterranean. The repertory was enormous, with designs such as guilloches, rhomboids, chevrons, ivy scrolls, key patterns, meanders, palmettes, peltae, wave crests, etc. This superb pavement, raised up as a wall, in the garden of the museum, is an innovative composition based on a grid of squared units, which is rich with textural motifs and colour.

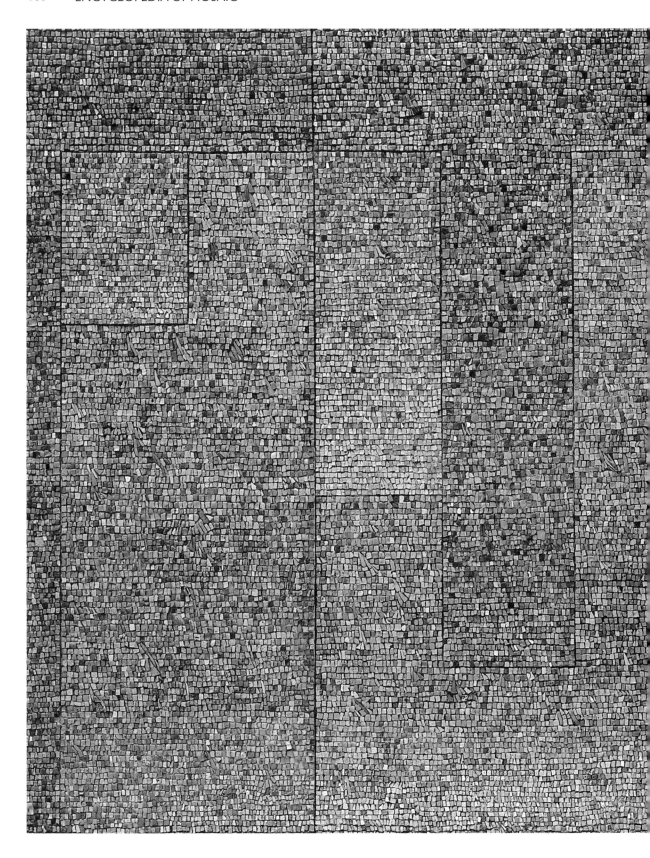

Tessera
Le Mura di Atlantide, 2001 by Marco De Luca, 174cm x 126cm / 68in x 50in, smalti, Venetian gold.

The Italian artist Marco De Luca (b. 1949) studied at the Istituto d'Arte per il Mosaico in Ravenna and at the Accademia di Belle Arti in Bologna. He lives and works in Ravenna, Italy. His works, constructed of fragments of materials, often in large areas of fairly uniform tesserae, are like poems of light constructed of their own inimitable syntax and inner rhythms. This work, again characterized by an almost Classical placing of regularly sized tesserae in opus tessellatum, is wondrously deceptive as any normally produced stasis is dissolved by such a placing into a surface like that of the sea, evoking movement, transparency and lucidity.

THEME The basic subject matter of a work and therefore its genre, e.g. marine, Nilotic (popular in Roman times), mythological, etc.

THERMAE (Latin) Roman baths (cf. It. *terme*).

THUMB-NAIL SKETCH A very small, very rough drawing (often for use as a visual aid).

TILE-BACKER BOARD A mineral fibreboard providing a rigid backing for mosaics in wet conditions, e.g. shower cubicles.

TILE CUTTERS There is a wide variety of cutters, which range from a simple glass or tile scorer to an electrical tile cutting machine. With the former, run the scorer directly on the tile alongside a metal rule or straight edge, then place the tile over the edge of a work table with the scored line directly above the edge and apply equal pressure on either side of the line with both hands. The tile will make a clean break.

TILE GRAFFITI A particularly common feature on buildings and street furniture in New York, where artists use tiles to form bold statements on columns, traffic lights and public benches.

TILE PRESS A machine that presses clay at great pressure to form a tile.

TILER'S SPONGE A large, dense sponge with a fine absorbing quality. **See *builder's sponge.***

TILES These may be unglazed or glazed, and can be found in a wide variety of colours, surface textures and thicknesses. Wall tiles can be cut using mosaic nippers, whereas floor tiles often need the help of a tile cutter.

TIMBER An excellent material for backing mosaics. It can be cut and shaped to size. When used for flooring, board over with plywood 12mm / $^1/_2$in thick, in the opposite direction to beams, and screw down to form a firm, flat surface to take a mosaic. **See *wood; plywood.***

TIN GLAZE A lead glaze with added tin oxide, resulting in an opaque white finish.

TIN LEAF Used in place of silver in Byzantine times as it was non-tarnishing. The top surface was varnished or painted in yellow to imitate gold.

TONAL CONTRASTS The relationships of lights to darks and vice versa.

TONE All colour has a tonal value, ranging between very pale and very dark grey. For accurate tonal value, imagine or create a black and white photograph; colours will be portrayed in degrees of grey, which is their tonal value. In practice it is the relative lightness or darkness found in a mosaic.

TRACING PAPER Thin transparent paper used over a drawing to copy it. Greaseproof or wax paper and plastic may also be utilized in copy work.

Tiles
Sculptural Surface (detail) – main entrance, Park Güell, Barcelona, Spain by Antoni Gaudí, 1900–03. (EMG)

The Spanish artist and architect Antoni Gaudí (1852–1926) was born in Reus in Spain. He studied at the School for Architecture in Barcelona and began a career in civic architecture from 1883 to 1900 in which he established the foundations of a unique and very personal style that flowered during the years 1900 to 1917 as seen in Casa Batlló, Casa Milá, the church of the Güell Colony and the Güell Park. The Güells were a wealthy Catalonian family who commissioned Gaudí to create a residential garden suburb. Gaudí employed many innovative ideas in his creation. He used reinforced concrete throughout, much of which was prefabricated and assembled on site (domes, the well-known 'serpentine' bench, entrance pavilions and colonnades), and all finished in cement, which invited a new surface treatment – external mosaic. This he created with an indigenous product – the tile – to bring colour and texture into the garden. All manner of tiles are in the garden – textured, patterned, glazed, unglazed and relief tiles – and have provided an inspiration for many a later visiting artist and mosaicist, most notably Niki de St Phalle.

TRAIL A strand of glass that is roughly circular in section. It is drawn out from a gather or unit of glass. **See** f*ilato.*

TRANSFER PRINTING The process of transferring a printed image by thin paper or gelatinous 'bats' to the surface of a tile before firing. When working with modern ceramics or tiles on external murals be aware that any 'transfers' that may appear permanent on the materials may be deceptive and come away in prolonged inclement weather.

TRANSFERRING The moving of a drawing or a design from a sketch format to the working base, e.g. (1) **Squaring up** – this usually involves enlarging a drawing. Draw a grid on the sketch and a grid on the working base in a proportional ratio; copy by freehand the main lines or areas square by square from sketch to base, then work up the final drawing, ignoring the grid. (2) **Photocopying** – this can enlarge, decrease/diminish, and concentrate on particular areas. The finished result can be applied to the base, traced or squared up. (3) **Ravenna-style** – trace the main lines or components on to a sheet of tracing paper. Ink these over on the reverse side and place on moist plaster or cement, etc., to leave an imprint of the design. (4) **Tracing** – use carbon or graphite paper to copy the drawings. (5) **Pouncing** – fix the drawing or cartoon to the floor, board or wall, and prick through the outline of the design using a prodder or sharp tool. Then brush over the holes with chalk dust, powder, charcoal dust, or colour wash, and remove the drawing/cartoon. Join the dots and work up into a good design.

TRANSLUCENT (of glass) Allowing light through, but not enough for objects to be seen clearly.

TRANSLUCENT MOSAIC WORK Uses stained glass or translucent vitreous mosaic tesserae. They are held in place with colourless epoxy resins on a glass or perspex base, and then grouted in place of leading (as in traditional stained glassmaking). Sometimes they can be encased in clear glass or vinyl on one or both sides, and used as panes of glass for windows or doors, or mounted and hung as 3D sculptures in conditions that maximize the through light. Called crystal glass mosaic, this method can also use transparent smalti.

TRANSPARENT (of glass or tile) That can be seen through. Some vitreous glass mosaic, which comes in an increasingly large colour range, is popularly used in mosaic making.

TRANSPARENT SMALTI A range of smalti made in Murano, Venice, for use in light-diffusing mosaic work, or to create specific effects; also known as trasparenti. The colour range is good and growing.

TRAVERTINE A light-coloured limestone commonly used for buildings around Rome and also in mosaic work.

TREE OF LIFE An image often used as a mosaic motif. The popular symbol is of a tree with leaves and/or flowers and fruits, often without a root. The Tree of Life may be interpreted in the Christian religion as both a symbol of knowledge and of life with contradictory values of negative and positive, vice and virtue. It illustrates the story of Man in a logical progression from the beginnings of time with Adam and Eve to Judgement Day. It is also found in many other religions as a strong moral symbol. The 12th-century pavimental mosaics in Puglia, Italy, use these themes, with fabulous renditions of human figures and beasts and explanatory words; e.g. Taranto, Cathedral of San Cataldo (1160), Trani Cathedral (c. 1165), Brindisi Cathedral (1163–65), and Otranto Cathedral (1163–65). *(Illustrated on pages 172–173)*

TRELLIS A network pattern used in mosaic for decorative borders and friezes.

TRENCADÍS A mosaic of glass and discarded fragments from the ceramic industry – *trencadís de ceràmica* – as used by Josep M Jujol in Parc Güell, Barcelona, Spain.

TRICLINIUM The dining area in a Classical Roman villa, with an arrangement of three couches, often around a mosaic emblema.

TROMPE L'OEIL This is an artistic illusion that 'deceives the eye'. A mosaic using naturalism may deceive the eye into thinking it is the real thing. It may be a mosaic of a picture, a perspectival view or a surface; e.g. the use of marble tesserae to look like

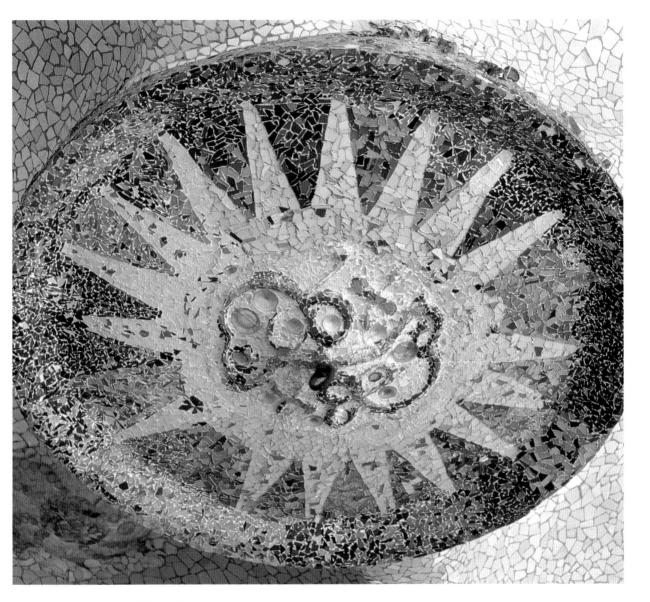

Trencadis
Trencadis – rosette (detail), 1911, Josep M Jujol, Park Güell, Barcelona, Spain. (EMG)

The Catalan artist and architect, Josep Maria Jujol (1879–1949) was born in
Tarragona and attended the Escuela de Arquitectura in Barcelona where he came
into contact with both the Art and Crafts movement and Art Nouveau. He formed
a remarkable relationship with the older Gaudí, becoming his assistant (1907) until
the latter's death. Encouraged by his master, it is him we have to thank for the
introduction of coloured shards of glass and ceramic in Gaudí's work, and above all
for the mosaic work at the Park Güell, including the serpentine bench, which was
decorated with waste from the ceramics industry. In the colonnaded walkway
beneath the serpentine bench the artist created an extraordinary array of rosettes,
at the place where some of the pillars would have engaged with the ceiling. They
were constructed with trencadis – an amalgam of recycled pottery, bottle glass,
tentacle-shaped glass and china – an extraordinary collage both surreal and
beautiful, and a forerunner to modern mosaic incorporating discarded elements
for aesthetic effect.

Tree of Life
Tree of Life (detail), Adam and Eve, The Temptation, Otranto Cathedral, Puglia, Italy, 12th century. (EMG)

The Otranto Cathedral has a mosaic on its floor that covers the nave and aisles. It is like a richly embroidered prayer rug, constructed of polychrome local limestone tesserae in lively naïve style. It is the masterpiece of the priest and artist Pantaleone, created between 1163 and 1165, and covers 600 square metres. The subject matter is a Christian representation of the Tree of Life, which begins in the nave and spreads its trunk and branches almost as far as the apse. It comprises a fantastic medieval bestiary, stories from Genesis in the Bible, the months of the year, Christian symbolism and heroic figures including Alexander the Great and King Solomon. In the transept is a depiction of Adam and Eve, each within a decorative roundel separated by a trunk of the tree containing the serpent. Both Adam and Eve hold the forbidden fruit, illustrative of original sin, and branches between their legs allude humorously to their new-found condition!

real marble, as in a floor made to resemble green onyx marble, Carthage, 4th century AD, Tunisia. **See also *lisibility*.**

TROWELS   Indispensable tools that come in various sizes and shapes. They are used in mosaic for rendering walls and floors and preparing cement bases. For levelling use straight-edged, long, metal trowels; for adhesives use notched, straight edged, or metal trowels; for grouting use rubber or plastic trowels and spreaders; and for spreading cement or adhesive use a variety, including mason's (pointed), plasterer's (square-ended), and pointing (rounded) trowels. All find their use!

TUFA   A soft stone composed of compacted volcanic ash.

TUNGSTEN-TIPPED TOOLS   Include stone carving chisels which give longevity and strength and are also useful for removing errant tesserae firmly embedded in cement; and also cutting implements in the form of nippers, mosaic hammers, etc.

TURPENTINE   A natural resin from the sap of pine trees. It can be used as a binder but may cause discoloration in porous tesserae.

TWEEZERS   Excellent little tools for positioning, placing, fixing, adjusting and setting tesserae without disturbing adjacent pieces. The long-pronged dental variety are especially good, and also the long and short 'eyebrow' variety.

TYCHE   Fate or fortune, chance, luck, often personified in Classical Roman mosaics as the protectress of a city.

URUK (Erech; mod. Warka, in Iraq)   A 4th-millennium BC Mesopotamian city. The earliest mosaic known is from here and is a wall mosaic constructed of half columns. It is an early temple frontage of about 25m / 80ft, in the area of Sumeria. Baked clay or terracotta 'cone-like' pegs were made so that their pointed edges could be pressed into the mud wall, thus displaying their circular bases, painted in red, black and white and arranged in geometric banded patterns of triangles, rhomboids and zig-zags. Part of the wall can be seen in the State Museum in Berlin, Germany.

UTILITY KNIFE   An exceedingly useful knife with a handle or shaft that holds a retractable and removable replaceable blade. It can be of various lengths, sizes and shape. **See *craft knives*.**

V

VALUE The intensity of shade and light in a colour. In a mosaic high values are light and low values are dark. 'Value' can be understood on a system of 0 to 10, ranging from black to white.

VARNISH A top coating, often in liquid form (e.g. Lascaox fixative), which is brushed or sprayed on to the surface of a mosaic to give it protection and may heighten the colour. It is rarely necessary to apply a varnish to the surface of mosaic materials as most are very durable and are chosen because of their inherent surface values.

VASELINE When this is applied to wood, plywood or hardboard it will prevent concrete from sticking, as will other forms of heavy-duty grease or oil. Vaseline is useful when using a simple frame in the indirect mosaic for slab-making, as it releases the finished work with ease. **See *parting agent.***

VATICAN STUDIO (also Vatican School, Vatican Mosaic Workshop) The Pontifical Workshop for Mosaics was established in 1576 under the patronage of Pope Gregory XIII to work on the mosaics for St Peter's Basilica in Rome, Italy. At first

Vatican studio – reproduction demonstration
Vatican Studio, Italy, Mosaic master at work, 1990. (EMG)

The establishment of the Vatican mosaic workshop to replace the paintings in St Peter's, Rome, with a more durable material – i.e. mosaic – put into practice the dictum attributed to the painter Domenico Ghirlandaio that mosaic produced 'pittura per l'eternità', painting for eternity, and set in motion a decline in the art of mosaic. The emphasis was now placed on extreme copyist skill, and the essence of mosaic making – its play with light, its abstract qualities and its ensuing spiritualism – was lost as more than 28,000 colours of smalti were produced to render mosaic more naturalistic and painterly. Today the Vatican workshop continues to make copies of paintings, mostly religious. They work to reproduce accurately a work by using an intermediate working cartoon, building up the design with close scrutiny of a photograph of the original. Spontaneity and innate creativity is superseded by the misguided skill in producing mosaic by template.

the school was located near the Gregorian Chapel, and then moved to the Palace of the Archpriest and finally to the Courtyard of San Damaso. In the early 17th century, Pope Urban VIII initiated much work in the mosaic studio, primarily to copy the oil paintings of St Peter's and render them into a more durable material (micromosaic). The tendency in the 16th century to imitate painting encouraged the use of tiny tesserae in order to produce painterly effects. One such mosaicist working at this time was Marcello Provenzale da Cenna (1577–1639) who is credited with being an initiator of this art form, which developed into a fashion during the 19th century (**see *Gilbert Collection***). In 1727 Benedetto XIII founded the Studio del Mosaico in the Vatican Palace, a virtually unchanged institution that continues to produce mostly pictorial *filato* mosaics, reproduction work and translation from paintings into mosaic.

VAULT An arched roof or semicircular arched roof. The earliest known examples of coloured tesserae on a vault are in the mid-1st century BC Republican cryptoporticus under Hadrian's Villa at Tivoli, Italy.

VERMICULATUM Literally 'wormlike'; **see *opus vermiculatum.***

VICTORIAN MOSAIC In mid-19th century Europe there was a revival of interest in mosaic making after the 16th- and 17th-century decline in the use of mosaic. A new industrial age saw the introduction of innovative ways of manufacturing and setting mosaic. An indirect or reverse method of setting mosaic attributed to the Italian mosaic artist Gian Domenico Facchina was taken up by the Venetian entrepreneur Antonio Salviati. His company in Venice produced work that could be pre-assembled and fixed in the 'new' indirect method on temporary paper bases and shipped to France and England where it was used in churches, banks and institutions. These prefabricated mosaics tended to be rather flat in both format and design, often taking on a lifeless, rather academic quality, with rare exceptions.

VINYL / RESIN A thermoplastic material used in mosaic making as a binder with sand and brick or marble dust.

VIRGIL The Roman poet, 70–19 BC; author of the *Aeneid*, an epic poem in 12 books, and a source of inspiration for numerous classical mosaics.

VITRARIUS A glassmaker.

VITREOUS GLASS This material is also known as mosaic glass, vitreous mosaic, vitreous glass tiles, commercial glass tiles, pressed glass and glass mosaic. These are manufactured glass tiles (usually 20 x 20mm / $^3/_4$ x $^3/_4$in; 25 x 25mm / 1 x 1in; or 50 x 50mm / 2 x 2in square), uniform in size, and generally having bevelled edges. The smooth side is normally regarded as the face, often having a slight

Victorian mosaic
Albert Memorial (detail), 1867, London, England. (EMG)

Antonio Salviati (1816–90) with the help of Murano glassmaker Lorenzo Radi (1803–74) re-examined the composition of Venetian glass smalti, and elaborated a system of 'indirect' setting of mosaic on to a temporary paper base. From this point onwards mosaics could be studio-made and transported to their final situation, world-wide. This method revitalized an interest in mosaic work and nowhere more so than in France and Victorian England. The Albert Memorial in London's Kensington Gardens was one of the most celebrated monuments to arts and science in the Victorian era, bringing together architect, engineer, builder, sculptor and mosaicist. Mosaics were to be set into the gables of the high canopy that protected the sculpture of the deceased Prince Consort, beloved husband of Queen Victoria (1819–1901). John Richard Clayton and George Bell, renowned stained-glass designers, combined their skills to design the mosaics of four allegorical female figures personifying architecture, poetry, painting and sculpture. Salviati's firm executed the mosaics in the indirect method. This detail from 'Painting' shows a painter and his model, and was photographed by the author in 1997 from scaffolding at the time of an enormous conservation campaign, now completed.

surface texture to prevent slipping and to resist scratches. The underside is often grooved to help better adhesion, but it can also be used face up for textural effects. They are made mainly in Italy, Mexico and France, and the colour range is very wide, though they are often not as colour-intense or as reflective as smalti. Their grainy quality and relative cheapness give great appeal to mosaicists. The material is resistant to light, heat, frost, chemicals and thermal shock. Tiles are usually bought fixed to sheets of paper or net, which can be soaked off and the loose tesserae used individually. They are sold in both squared sheets and occasionally loose by weight. Some tiles have transparent adhesive film stuck to their surface that enables easy fixing, after which the film is gently pulled off. The variety of colours is widened by some types having mixed copper dust scattered into the molten form, resulting in a sparkling finish. These are known variously as metallic vitreous glass, aventurine glass, and bronzed glass. **See *aventurine.***

VITREOUS PASTE Coloured or colourless opaque or transparent glass, obtained by smelting and cooling a mixture of silica (the vitrifier), sand, flux and metal colouring oxides. The tesserae produced range in size from 3mm / $^1/_8$in to around 1cm / $^3/_8$in thick. **See *glass paste tesserae, smalto.***

VITRIFIED Non-porous (non-absorbing) – a quality of all mosaic glass.

VITRUVIUS A Roman writer of the late 1st century BC who gave instructions in his book on architecture for the preparation of a foundation for a pavement that can withstand weight, wet weather and frost without subsiding, which remain the basis or guideline for laying mosaic. On a level base of broken stones lay a layer of fairly large stones or pebbles; over this place a layer of broken bricks or stones and lime mortar up to approx. 20cm / 8in; over this a 2cm / $^3/_4$–1in layer of crushed tile and lime mortar, and then lay the mosaic pavement tesserae in a fine thin bed of lime, volcanic ash and marble dust. **See *nucleus; rudus; statumen.***

VOLUTE A popular decorative spiral form, used in decorative mosaic from the 5th century BC to the present day.

WALL Traditionally a wall to take mosaic consisted of three or four layers of mortar (see diagram). The final layer (*intonaco fresco*; fresh plaster), or butter coat, into which the tesserae would be set, was approx. 1–2cm / $^1/_2$–$^3/_4$ in thick and was applied just before the setting process. This top coat was prepared in quantities usable for one day's work. **See *giornata.***

WALL MOSAICS The earliest known mosaics were wall mosaics (see **Uruk**), which were a form of decorative covering for a mud wall and that also gave structural reinforcement. Later, walls were often coated with tar or resin as a setting mastic, and in cupolas or curved areas nails with slightly projecting flat heads were used as reinforcing armatures to hold the mortar binders. Mosaics were also used in ancient times on walls to decorate fountains and nymphaea in natural and (later) artificial grottoes using shells, glass and volcanic pumice as materials. Nowadays, cement adhesives can be applied directly to a wall of brick or stone, though a rendering of cement mortar is still advisable. Sometimes ceramic nails with grooved or threaded heads, or twisted loops of steel wire, are inserted into the wall to help anchor and hold the plaster and reinforce the plaster coat. *(Illustrated overpage)*

WALL TILES Usually of earthenware clay with a decorated glazed surface. They are generally thinner and more porous than floor tiles, and easier to cut.

WATER GILDING A method of adhering gold leaf to glass to create a permanent mirrored effect. Use any glass that is translucent or semitranslucent. Prop the glass at an angle and clean thoroughly using methylated spirits on a soft cloth. Make a size or glue. **Procedure**: Almost half-fill a glass jar with distilled water (45%) and fill just over half the remaining space (approximately 35%) with methylated spirits. Add about 1$^1/_2$ capsules of gelatine to the mix and gently heat it in a double boiler until the capsules disperse/dissolve; it should look glossy. Use 3–3$^1/_2$ capsules if applying white gold or palladium leaves; use 4–4$^1/_2$ gelatine capsules if applying aluminium or copper leaves. Apply the warm size to the glass using a soft brush. It will be necessary to pick up the fragile leaf with a squirrel-tip brush – a very fine gilder's brush – and apply it quickly and gently to the glass. An electric charge or static electricity created between the two surfaces will ensure adherence. If the glass is largish, work in strips along the top of the glass, overlapping at the joins. Clean any dribbled solution off the glass with methylated spirits before continuing to apply the leaf at lower levels. Leave to dry for up to 24 hours in a warm room. Any air bubbles that may be trapped can be gently tamped using a gilder's tip brush, and the gold will settle down smoothly. When dry, use a cotton bud to remove overlapping excess gold that has not adhered to the glass. The glass is then backed for protection in one or two ways: if the glass is to be cut into shapes, use a soft brush to apply a backing of oil paint slightly diluted with white spirit, and allow to dry for about 12 hours. If the glass is not to be cut, back it with a coat of sign writer's enamel paint. **See *'gold' glass; metallic foil.***

WATERSOLUBLE GLUES Also called hydro-adhesives. Adhesives that are dissolved in water and therefore not permanent, and are used in the indirect and double reverse methods of mosaic making, e.g. flour and water paste, gum arabic, fish glue.

WAVE CREST A decorative border of repeated shapes resembling the crests of waves. It was used from Greco–Roman times and is still popular.

WAX-RESIN GLUE A binder or adhesive made from beeswax or paraffin wax, used in Byzantine portable mosaics made up of tiny tesserae stuck to wood. It was also used as an adhesive at the Vatican workshop in the process for making miniature copies and small portative mosaic works.

WEATHERING The term for surface changes occurring on tiles, caused by chemical reaction with the environment.

WELDING IRON/TORCH A tool for joining metal to metal, and often used in assembling a structural armature.

WINDOW GLASS Also called plate glass, it can be used in mosaic as a backing support. It comes in a variety of thicknesses, generally 4–6mm / $^1/_8$–$^1/_4$ in. When applying mosaic tesserae, use adhesives that dry clear. Great play can be made of coloured grouts, as these will be given added emphasis when held against the light. **See *stained glass.***

THE CROSS SECTION
OF A BYZANTINE WALL MOSAIC

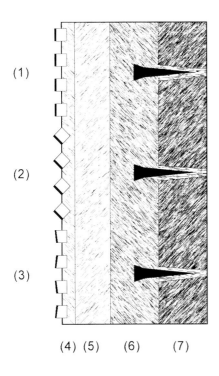

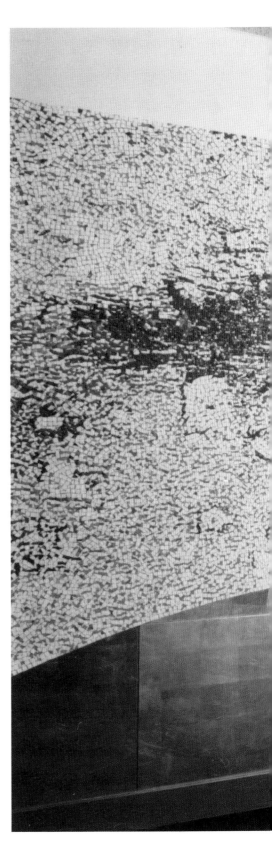

(1) Gold tesserae set uniformly flat into the butter coat (4)

(2) Gold tesserae set at a regular angle into the butter coat

(3) Gold tesserae set at varying angles into the butter coat

(4) The butter coat: fine setting bed

(5) A moderately fine mortar layer

(6) A coarse mortar layer

(7) The brick wall into which reinforcing nails were fixed
    to provide a better grip for the coarse mortar

**Wall mosaics –
Toyoharu Kii**
Wind Blows, 1997 by
Toyoharu Kii, 2.5m x
10m / 98in x 400in,
marble, smalti,
aluminium foil.

The Japanese artist
Toyoharu Kii (b. 1953)
was born in Ehime, and
studied at the National
University of Fine Arts
and Music in Tokyo. A
prolific and versatile
artist, he specializes in
wall or mural mosaics,
having completed over
50. This mural embodies
the artist's credo that
the mosaic should be
like a skin on an
architectural support,
one that embraces pure
aesthetic. The materials
and their inherent
qualities are paramount,
both in the light-
emitting surface of glass
and foils, and in the rich
and uneven textures
created by marble.
Enjoyment of surface is
to the fore.

WOOD An obvious base for a mosaic. Plywood, of external or marine quality, is suitable for most indoor work and can be cut, shaped or assembled to any size or form. Waterseal the cut edges and the surface if necessary. Keep flat and dry when storing, and vary the thickness according to the size of the work. Other woods, including hard woods, can be used to frame finished works. Choose woods of empathic colours and grain. See *timber.*

WORKSHOP A team of artists and/or artisans working together in a studio. The best known are in Italy and include the Academia di Belle Arti di Ravenna (workshop/school); Akomena Spazio Mosaico, Ravenna (workshop/artisans); Associazione Mosaicisti di Ravenna (workshop/artisans); Bisazza Mosaico, near Vicenza (laboratories/ artisans); Cooperativa Mosaicisti di Ravenna (artisans); Scuola Mosaicisti del Friuli, Spilimbergo (school); 'Gino Severini' Istituto Statale d'Arte, Ravenna (school); and Angelo Orsoni snc, Venice (workshop/artisans).

Window glass
Nut, 2000 by Rebecca Newnham, Swan Centre, Leatherhead, England, 2.5m x 1.25m / 98in x 45in, glass, enamel.

This commissioned panel was one of five made by the English artist Rebecca Newnham for placement in Surrey, England. Each panel contains a botanical quotation from a locally revered poet or writer. The artist and nonsense poet Edward Lear was the inspiration for this panel, an illustrative work featuring five types of nut. The base of the panel is window glass, painted with enamel and lustre and kiln-fired before the 'mosaic' glass is applied.

Workshop
Workshop of the company of Angelo Orsoni snc, Venice 1999.

The photograph shows the author with the Venetian artist Lucio Orsoni on the left and his personal assistant on the right. The painting behind Elaine's head is of Angelo Orsoni, the great-grandfather of Lucio and founder of the workshop in 1888. The workshop is world-renowned in producing smalti glass and Venetian gold.

XENIA The 'friendly gifts' that passed between host and guest in Classical times. These gave rise to popular motifs for the mosaic-decorated floors of the *triclinium* (dining room) or *oecus* (large reception room) in a Roman villa, such as baskets of grapes, figs and dates, braces of edible birds, or fish, etc. Today small mosaic panels are popularly made for kitchen and dining area walls and floors by many mosaicists.

ZELLIJ (zelliges) Moroccan mosaic, constructed of handmade, hand-glazed and hand-cut tiles, or *furmah*, which are equivalent to tesserae. Derived from the Byzantine and Roman tradition of mosaics, they are nowadays used for wall panels, archways, fountains, stairways, columns, mirrors and fireplaces. The tiles consist of a repertoire of pre-cut shapes, forming stars, honeycombs, webs, steps, chequerboards, etc. The clays and glazes are local to the areas where they are made, in particular the royal cities of Meknès and Fez. After first scoring the lines, a tile cutter or *taksir nqaash* cuts the tiles, using a chisel-headed hammer, sharpened on both sides, against a steel anvil, just like a hammer and hardie. The glazed end of the tile holds the patterns, and the end to be embedded is tapered. A layout artist or *fraasj* and his assistants (*zlayji*) create the pattern face down on paper, on which the design has been partially drawn (allowing for natural imprecision) with outlines traced with an *udel khizran* or bamboo stick dipped in ink. When completed the tiles are walked on – gingerly – to press or tamp them down, and a powdered cement is sprayed over the design, followed the next day by a 7cm / 3in concrete backing. This very heavy panel is then lifted and attached to the wall or permanent base, where the intricate and beautiful coloured panel is first seen.

Zellij
Zellij, Marrakech, Morocco, 2002, courtyard fountain (detail) in 'Dar Aicha', home and studio of author Elaine M Goodwin. (JM)

Morocco has an active tradition of decorative mosaic work – zellij – which was first developed in Moorish Spain. Because it is in a Muslim country, the designs rely for their impact on geometric decoration and draw attention away from the real world to pure form. Geometric decoration presents a direct analogy to spiritual truths, a clear two-dimensional order. Many designs seem kaleidoscopic in colour and design, but all lead to a hidden point, a single point – the Creator. This simple, single-coloured fountain design uses the star as its geometric image and the author, whose house this fountain is in, has used this image to inspire her work there.

Suppliers

The author gratefully acknowledges the following companies and suppliers for their technical expertise and help in compiling this encyclopaedia.

FRANCE

Opio Colour *vitreous glass*
4 Route de Cannes
06650 Opio
France
tel +33 (0)4 92 60 32 22 / fax +33 (0)4 92 60 32 20
email opio@opiocolor.com
www.opiocolor.com

ITALY

Bisazza spa *vitreous glass*
36041 Alte
Vicenza
Italy
tel + 39 0444 707 511 / fax + 39 0444 492 088

Mario Donà e Figli snc *smalti*
Via Marchetti
4–6 Zona Artigianale
I-33097 Spilimbergo (PN)
Italy
tel +39 0427 51125 / fax +39 0427 927 786
email vetreriadona@libero.it
www.mosaico.net/mariodona

Ferrari & Bacci snc *marble*
Via Aurelia 14
55045 Pietrasanta (LU)
Italy
tel +39 0584 790147 / fax +39 0584 794182
email info@fbmosaic.com
www.fbmosaic.com

Mosaici Donà Murano *smalti, transparents*
Fdm. Venier 38/a
30141 Murano (VE)
Italy
tel +39 041 736 596 / fax +39 041 739 969
email info@mosaicidona.com
www.mosaicidona.com

Angelo Orsoni snc *Venetian gold, smalti,*
Cannaregio 1045/A *hammer, hardie*
30121 Venezia
Italy
tel +39 041 244 0003 / fax +39 041 524 0736
email info@orsoni.com
www.orsoni.com

Ravennae srl *Ravenna gold*
Viale Scalo di S. Lorenzo 40
00185 Rome
Italy
tel +39 0644 50070 / fax +39 0644 56760
email y2k@tabularasa.com
www.tabularasa.com

Sicis *special glass tile smalti*
Via Manlio Mont. 9/11
48100 Ravenna
Italy
tel +39 0544 451 340 / fax +39 0544 451 464

UNITED KINGDOM

Bisazza UK Ltd *vitreous glass*
Unit 18
Boundary Business Court
92–94 Church Road
Mitcham, Surrey CR4 3TD
tel +44 (0)20 86 40 79 94 / fax +44 (0)20 86 40 56 64

Chris Blanchett *mosaic books, historical,*
Buckland Books *contemporary*
Holly Tree House
18 Woodlands Road
Littlehampton, W Sussex BN17 5PP
tel / fax +44 (0)1903 717 648
email c.blanchett@lineone.net

L Cornelissen & Son Ltd *pigments, gold leaf*
105 Great Russell Street
London WC1B 3RY
tel +44 (0)20 76 36 10 45 /
fax +44 (0)20 76 36 36 55
email info@cornelissen.com
www.cornelissen.com

Paul Fricker *glass, ceramic, tools, adhesives*
452 Pinhoe Road
Exeter EX4 8HN
tel +44 (0)1392 468 440 / fax + 44 (0)1392 468 447
email paulfrickerltd@aol.com
www.mosaicsbymailorder.co.uk

James Hetley & Co. Ltd *stained glass, nippers*
Glasshouse Fields *(wheel), glass baubles*
London E1W 3J4
tel +44 (0)20 7790 2333 / fax +44 (0)20 7790 0201
email tad@idesglass.co.uk
www.hetleys.co.uk

Mapei (UK) Lt *adhesives, grouts*
4 Waterfront Business Park
Dudley Road,
Brierley Hill,
West Midlands DY5 1LX
tel +44 (0)1384 483 900 / fax +44 (0)1384 483 200

Mosaic Workshop *mosaic materials*
Unit B,
443-449 Holloway Road
London N7 6LJ

also at
1a Princeton Street
London WC1R 4AX
tel / fax +44 (0)20 7272 2446
email: sales@mosaicworkshop.com
www.mosaicworkshop.com

Opals (Mirror-Flex) Company Ltd *mosaic*
14a Herbert Road *materials*
Clacton-on-Sea
Essex CO15 3BE
tel + 44 (0)1255 423 927 / fax +44 (0)1255 221 117
email sales@mirrorflex.co.uk
www.mirrorflex.co.uk

Reed Harris *Cinca ceramic, tools,*
Riverside House *glass, adhesives*
27 Carnwath Road
London SW6 3HR
tel +44 020 7736 7511 / fax +44 020 7736 2988
email enquiries@reed-harris.co.uk
www.reedharris.co.uk

Sureset UK Ltd., *resin surfaces*
Unit 32
Deverll Road Trading Estate
Sutton Verry
Warminster,
Wiltshire BA12 7BZ
tel + 44 (0)1985 841 180 / fax + 44 (0)1985 841 260
email mail@sureset.co.uk
www.sureset.co.uk

Alec Tiranti Ltd
27 Warren Street *armatures, ciment*
London W1T 5NB *fondu, hammers, resins*
tel + 44 (0)20 7636 8565
email
enquiries@tiranti.co.uk
www.tiranti.co.uk

also at
Alec Tiranti,
70 High Street
Theale
Reading, Berkshire RG7 5AR
tel + 44 (0)118 930 2775 / fax + 44 (0)118 932 3487

Tower Ceramics Ltd *mosaic tiles, netting*
91 Parkway
Camden Town
London NW1 7PP
tel +44 (0)20 74 85 71 92 / fax +44 (0)20 72 67 95 71

Edgar Udny & Co. Ltd   smalti, gold, vitreous,
The Mosaic Centre   cement, adhesives
314 Balham High Road
London SW17 7AA
tel +44 (0)20 8767 8181 / fax +44 (0)20 8767 7709

Unibond   adhesives
Henkel Home Improvement
& Adhesive Products
Winsford
Cheshire CW7 3QF
tel +44 (0)1606 593 933

Wellington Tile Company   glass tiles,
Tont Estate, Milverton Road   including Mexican
Wellington
Somerset TA21 0A2
tel +44 (0)1823 667 242 / fax +44 (0)1823 665 685

also at
161 St Johns Hill,
Clapham Junction
London SW11
tel +44 (0)20 79 24 17 80

USA

Cajun Enterprises   *free-standing universal*
2517 Lawrence Drive   *cutter, stone mosaics*
Meraux
LA 70075
USA
tel / fax +1 0504 279 7554
email mosaicstonesupply@bigfoot.com
www.mosaicstonesupply.com

Selected bibliography

The Art of Mosaic, Catalogue, Associates of the Los Angeles County Museum of Art, 1977.

Ashton, et al., **The Mosaics of Jeanne Reynal** (contributions by Ashton, Campbell, Tyler, de Kooning, Pfriem and Reynal), New York, October House, Inc., 1969.

Berry, John, **Making Mosaics**, London, Studio Vista, 1966.

Buckton, David, ed., **Byzantium; Treasures of Byzantine Art and Culture**, The Trustees of the British Museum, 1994.

Carabatea, Marilena, **Greek Mythology**, Adam Editions, 1997.

Cimok, Fatih, ed., **Antioch Mosaics**, pub. A Turizm Yayinlari, Turkey, 2000.

Cordello, **Guide to the Ruins of Ostia**, Edizioni Storti, 1988.

Dennis, Lisl and Landt, **Living in Morocco**, London, Thames and Hudson 2001

Dorigo, Wladimiro, **Late Roman Painting**, London, J M Dent, 1971.

Dunbabin, Katherine M D, **Mosaics of the Greek and Roman World**, Cambridge, Cambridge University Press, 1999.

Farnetti, Manuela, **Glosario Technico-storico del Mosaico**, Ravenna, Longo Editore, 1993.

Fassett, Kaffe and Candace Bahouth, **Mosaics**, Ebury Press, 1999.

Fiorentini Roncuzzi, Isotta and Elisabetta Fiorentini, **Mosaic – Materials, Techniques and History**, Ravenna, MWEV Editions, 2002.

Fiorucci, Gabriela, **Mosaic: The Work of the Muses**, Pascarelli, 2000.

Fischer, Peter, **Mosaic; History and Technique**, London, Thames and Hudson, 1971.

Fuks, Paul, **Picassiette – le Jardin d'Assiettes**, Neuchâtel, Editions Ides et Calendes, 1992.

Garnett, Angelica, **Mosaics**, Oxford, Oxford University Press, 1967.

Gaudí, text and publishing, Barcelona, Escudo de Oro, 1990.

Goodwin, Arthur (with contributions by E M Goodwin), **The Technique of Mosaic**, London, Batsford, 1985.

Goodwin, Elaine M, **Decorative Mosaic**, London, Letts/New Holland, 1996.

_____**The Art of Decorative Mosaic**, Marlborough, Wilts., Crowood, 1999.

_____**Classic Mosaic**, London, Apple, 2000.

Harden, Donald B, **Glass of the Caesars**, Milan, Olivetti, 1987.

Harvey, Hazel, **Discovering Exeter 9 / Community Mosaics**, Exeter, Exeter Civic Society, 1998.

Henig, Martin, ed., **A Handbook of Roman Art**, Oxford, Phaidon, 1983.

Herbert, Tony and Kathryn Huggins, **The Decorative Tile in Architecture and Interiors**, Phaidon, 1995.

Howarth, Maggy, **The Art of Pebble Mosaic**, Search Press, 1994.

Kondoleon, Christine, **Antioch: The Lost Ancient City**, Princeton University Press, 2001.

Kourkoutidou-Nikolaidou, E, **Wandering in Byzantine Thessaloniki**, Kapon Editions, 1997.

Lauppi, Walter, **Mosaics with Natural Stones**, Sterling, 1974.

Lessing, Erich and Antonio Varone, **Pompeii**, Paris, Terrail, 1995.

Ligtelijn, Vincent, and Rein Saariste, **Josep M Jujol**, Rotterdam, OIO Publishers, 1996.

Ling, Roger, **Roman Painting**, Cambridge, Cambridge University Press 1991.

_____**Ancient Mosaics**, London, British Museum Press, 1998.

L'Orange, H P and P J Nadhagen, **Mosaics**, London, Methuen, 1966.

Mellentin Haswell, J, **Mosaics**, London, Thames and Hudson, 1973.

Mills, John, **Encyclopaedia of Sculpture Techniques**, London, B T Batsford, 2001.

Moldi Ravenna, Cristiana, **I Colori della Luce; Angelo Orsoni e l'arte del mosaico**, Marsilio Editori, 1996.

Neal, David S, **Roman Mosaics in Britain**, London,

Alan Sutton Publishing Ltd, 1981.

Nittolo, Felice, **Un Sogno di Mosaico**, privately published, 2000.

Oakeshott, Walter, **The Mosaics of Rome**, London, Thames and Hudson, 1967.

Pajares-Ayuela, Paloma, **Cosmatesque Ornament**, London, Thames and Hudson, 2002.

Pascarelli, Gabriella Fiorucci, **Mosaic; the Work of the Muses**, 2000, n.p. ISBN 88-900425-0-8.

Pegoraro, Silvia, ed., **Oggetti del Desiderio**, exhibition catalogue, Electra, 1997.

Permanym, Lluís, **Gaudì of Barcelona**, Ediciones Polígrafa SA., 1997.

Ramage, Nancy H and Andrew Ramage, **The Cambridge History of Roman Art**, Cambridge, Cambridge University Press, 1991.

Rediscovering Pompeii, catalogue, l'Erma di Bretscheider, 1992.

Rossi, Fernando, **Mosaics**, London, Pall Mall Press, 1970.

San Casciani, Paul, **The Technique of Decorative Stained Glass**, London, B T Batsford, 1985 (reprinted 2000).

Scuola di Mosaico e Mosaici, Spilimbergo, catalogue, Italy, 1997.

Spadoni, Claudio and Isotta Fiorentini, **Frammenti di un Discorso Musivo**, Charta (Italy), 1999.

Strong, Donald and David Brown, eds, **Roman Crafts**, Duckworth and Co., 1976.

Suter, Caroline and Celia Gregory, **The Art of Mosaic**, Anness Publishing Ltd, 2001.

Tammisto, Antero, **Birds in Mosaics**, Acta Institui Romani Finlandiae, 1997.

Tiranti, Alec, **The Polyester Resin Booklet**, Alec Tiranti Ltd, 2000.

_____**Casting in Ciment Fondu**, Alec Tiranti Ltd, 1999.

Unger, Hans, **Practical Mosaics**, London, Studio Vista, 1965.

Vitruvius, **On Architecture**, Book 7.

Walter-Kasydi, Elena, **The Greek House**, The Archaeological Society at Athens, 1998.

Ward-Perkins, John and Amanda Claridge, **Pompeii**, AD79, Alfred A Knopf, 1978.

Whitemore, Thomas, **The Mosaics of Hagia Sophia at Istanbul**, Oxford University Press, 1952.

Woodford, Susan, **The Cambridge Introduction to Art: Greece and Rome**, Cambridge, Cambridge University Press, 1982.

Yegül, Fikret, **Baths and Bathing in Classical Antiquity**, Architectural History Foundation & Massachusetts Institute of Technology, 1992.

Photo credits

Most of the photos in this book are by John Melville (credited as JM) or the author (credited as EMG). All possible efforts have been made to achieve accreditation for photographs; when no response has been forthcoming, apologies are offered for any consequent omissions.

Photographs of individual artists' work are by the artists themselves, except for: K. Budd (**Oliver Budd**); Francis Goëller (**Pascale Beauchamps**); Giora Shafir (**Ilana Shafir**); Norbert Heyl (**Lucio Orsoni**); Daniele Casadio (**Stefano Mazzotti**); Banzola-Faenza (**Felice Nittolo**); J P Thoury (**Henry-Noël Aubry**); Shona Wood (**Tessa Hunkin**); Vanni Mulinaris (**Giovanna Galli**); Ekta (**Fabrice Vannier**); Gilles Duchesneau (**Mireille Lévesque**); Paolo Solitro (**Marco De Luca**); Akio Suzuki (**Toyoharu Kii**); David Bird (**Rebecca Newnham**).

Special mention and gratitude to Demetrios Chrysopoulos for permission to photograph in Daphni Monastery, Athens, and Professor Charalambos Bakirtzis and the Department of Culture in Thessaloniki for allowing me to photograph in the Rotonda of Hosios Giorgios in Thessaloniki; also to the Royal Albert Memorial Museum and Art Gallery in Exeter, and to the Birmingham Museums and Art Gallery.

Special mention is made of the following:
BAMM – The British Association for Modern Mosaic, President, Elaine M Goodwin. Membership enquiries to: The Membership Secretary, 15 Hillside Avenue, Exeter EX4 4NW, UK.
Or email: r.m.ayubi@ex.ac.uk
For information about BAMM, visit website: www.bamm.org.uk

SAMA – The Society of American Mosaic Artists
For details, email: info@americanmosaics.org
Or write to: SAMA, P.O. Box 428, Orangeburg, SC29116, USA.
Or visit website:
www.americanmosaics.org/contacts.html

MAAJ – The Mosaic Artists Association of Japan
For details, email: kii@ttv.ne.jp
Or write to: MAAJ, c/o Ichiro Kodama, 5-18-11-802, Negisi, Taito-ku, Tokyo, 110-0003 Japan.
Or visit website: www.bbig.or.jp/~mosaic.jp

Australia: For details, contact Nola Diamantoupoulos, tel. +00 61 9818 7471, Rozelle, Australia.

Worldwide: The International Association of Contemporary Mosaicists / Associazione Internazionale Mosaicisti Contemporanei (AIMC).

For details, contact: Rosanna Fattorini, Via di Roma 13, 48100 Ravenna, Italy, tel/fax + 39 0544 215 004.

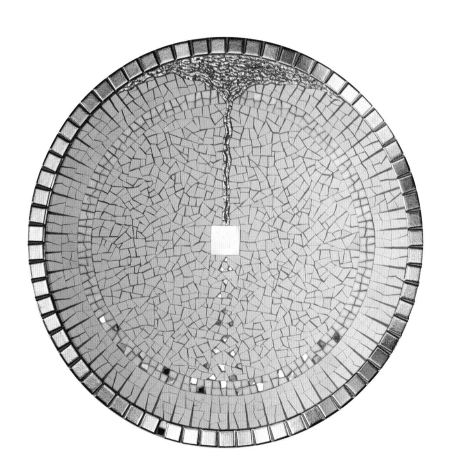